POSITIVE
MIND POWER

POSITIVE MIND POWER
Lessons From Real Life

RAKESH K MITTAL

A Sterling Paperback

STERLING PAPERBACKS
An imprint of
Sterling Publishers (P) Ltd.
A-59, Okhla Industrial Area, Phase-II,
New Delhi-110020.
Tel: 26387070, 26386209; Fax: 91-11-26383788
E-mail: sterlingpublishers@airtelmail.in
ghai@nde.vsnl.net.in
www.sterlingpublishers.com

Positive Mind Power
Lessons From Real Life
© Rakesh K. Mittal
ISBN 978-81-207-2894-3
Reprint 2006, 2007, 2008, 2012

All rights are reserved.
No part of this publication may be reproduced, stored in a retrieval system or transmitted, in any form or by any means, mechanical, photocopying, recording or otherwise, without prior written permission of the original publisher.

Printed and Published by Sterling Publishers Pvt. Ltd., New Delhi-110 020.

*This book is dedicated
to my all teachers
who imparted knowledge and
wisdom to me.
This made my life positive.*

FOREWORD

It is with immense pleasure and profit that I have gone through the collection of Shri Rakesh Mittal's articles now being brought out in book form as *Positive Mind Power*.

I first came to know Rakesh in 1975 when he was beginning his IAS career at the Lal Bahadur Shastri National Academy of Administration, of which I was the Director at that time. While I was engaged in guiding his first steps in public administration, I had little thought that the time would come when he would be helping to guide my own steps in the far more vast and wider field of life. But that is exactly what I feel after reading this series of articles and deriving so many valuable lessons in tackling life's problems.

As he rightly says, **"Happiness is a state of mind and the goal of human life is to attain that state of mind."** And that is precisely what this book helps us to do. It is full of practical wisdom drawn from even the most ordinary day-to-day episodes. The most striking feature about Rakesh is his positive approach to life and its manifold problems. From that point of view the book has been very well named. Most of us, seeing the extent of ills and weaknesses in our present-day society keep bemoaning the fact without being able to assert ourselves to do something about them. But Rakesh refuses to be overwhelmed by these evils and urges us to stand up and fight them, and is confident that they can be contained, if not overcome. He rightly stresses that for this, our own right conduct and approach is essential. It is this positive approach to life and to society in general that led him to found the Kabir Peace Mission, which is working precisely for the attainment of these objectives.

In addition to his positive outlook is his practical approach to problems. He is able to draw valuable lessons from even routine activities. In a number of places, he cleverly compares life to flying in an aeroplane, and then goes on to remind us that even while flying high, we have to keep in mind that ultimately we have to come to the ground. This is a sentiment also beautifully expressed in the lines of a Hindi poet :

पंछी भले तुम छू लो छत व्योम की,
धरा पर तुम्हें लौट आना ही होगा।

At another point he compares learning to grapple with life's problems with learning and mastering the various steps in horse riding, and makes very striking comparisons. Elsewhere, he says life is like a game of tennis, and at another point he holds out the example of the Rubik cube. Even the ever-flowing Ganga induces in him the thought that just as the holiness of the Ganga lies in its flow, so our salvation lies not in hoarding Nature's gifts to us, but in letting them flow freely out to those in need.

One enviable gift which Rakesh has is his ability to put down his thoughts in writing then and there. Many of us, even when deeply moved and inspired and wanting very much to concretise these sentiments in writing, keep putting it off until the moment is gone and the opportunity is lost. Thus we fail to give some measure of continuity and permanency to our deepest thoughts and emotions, emotions that would be all the richer for being shared with others, thoughts that might well have helped and inspired many grappling with life's myriad problems.

A reading of these articles also reveals Rakesh's capacity to absorb great ideas and inspiration from inspiring books he has read or profound talks he has heard, and present the essence of these profound thoughts and inspiration in just a few well-chosen words. Not everyone of us may have the opportunity to read these books or listen to these talks, but we can share the wisdom and the inspiration through these presentations.

In a short foreword of this nature, it is not possible to do justice to the wealth of thoughts and ideas potrayed in this series of articles. They are a challenge to our better nature. If we could but adopt even some of these ideas and suggestions, it will help us to lead better lives and contribute to building a better society. That will be Rakesh Mittal's real reward.

54 EC Road,   **Rajeshwar Prasad**
Dehradun 248 001.   IAS (Retd.)

PREFACE

This book is a reproduction of my book *Positive Lessons from Life*. The book was first published in the year 1996 and contained lessons learnt by me from my own life.

Life is a mystery for all of us. Its course is so uncertain that every coming moment is an anxiety. But this uncertainity is exactly what makes it interesting. Looked in parts half of life is if (read the middle two alphabets) and three-fourth is 'lie' (read it without 'f'). Yet in totality it is the most wonderful opportunity and its course is determined by none else than us. In fact, we are the divine architect behind our life. Only fortunate few are able to understand this reality, others waste it in accusing their environment.

Life has been no different for me too. Like a rose flower, it has the beautiful petals as well as sharp thorns. I take them complementary to each other. This is what I have tried to reflect in this book. I learnt from all events of life, good or bad, but my learning has been positive. I feel that life, though may appear adhoc and arbitrary, is not so in reality. If we have a learning attitude and faith in nature, we start seeing a positive meaning in all events. In the process life gets enriched day by day leading to its real goal.

I believe in sharing all acquisitions including wisdom. I am not saying so with any sense of arrogance or superiority but with a deep sense of humility. Therefore, I am sharing my learning in the form of this book. The lessons have been kept in the same sequence in which they were written. As a result, they also reflect the process of ripening. It shall be my endeavour to keep sharing whatever is learnt by me from life.

Many have helped me in this work and I express my deep gratitude towards them. I am in particular grateful to Shri Rajeshwar Prasad, my Director at Lal Bahadur Shastri Academy of Administration, Mussoorie who very affectionately wrote 'Foreword' of the original book and the same has been reproduced in this book. I also bow my head in the holy feet of Swami Bhoomanandji whose association has clarified my doubts and who still continues to guide me in this vast ocean of life. May his blessings shower on me eternally.

'UPVAN' **Rakesh K Mittal**
1/14, Vishwas Khand,
Gomti Nagar,
Lucknow-226010
Phone : 0522-2309147
E-mail : rakesh_mittal_2000@yahoo.com

There are two kinds of people
in this world ....
Givers and Takers !
The Takers eat well ....
but the Givers sleep well !

BLESSINGS

Undoubtedly it is knowledge or education that distinguishes man from the rest of earth's creation. And it is the actual process of learning which each person undergoes that determines his knowledge. For providing education, we have set up schools, colleges, universities, research and training centres and the like. None the less, real learning always remains a process which everyone has to take up and pursue individually.

Does it therefore mean that learning necessarily depends upon some specific set of circumstances like place, facilities and the various means and procedures evolved for the purpose ? Or is there always scope for everyone to learn, no matter where he is and whatever are the factors surrounding him ? This is where practical and timely lessons from actual life become paramount.

Are people, including the scholarly and the educated, given to making use of their day to day life in the world in order, to become more resourceful and contented, marching towards a state of stability and fulfilment? Perhaps the answer is invariably no.

It is in this context that Rakesh K Mittal's presentation of 'Positive Learning from Life' becomes helpful, illustrative and even compulsive. No matter what level or station of life one belongs to, there is still every scope for him to learn and get enriched every day. Whether one's income is sufficient, facilities adequate, opposition stiff or risks and dangers immense, life holds ample scope to refine and moderate oneself at the sensory, mental and intellectual levels — and what more, at the core of spiritual level also, where alone the human has a full prospect of becoming happy, stable and fulfilled.

To think is the supreme quality of human life. But in thinking, the thinker must always have a clear objective of getting enriched and strengthened every time. Ensuring that this is so is the essence of positive thinking. Our mind is gifted by Nature with the great ability to look at every situation and person, interpret things and events, respond and react to any, episode or interaction in a beneficial, elevating manner,

In Treta Yuga in the palace of Ayodhya, Vasishtha gave an 18-day tuition to Sri Rama on how to handle the mind and intelligence making them unassailable in every way. One message in the dialogue stands out, sparkling even today as a great pointer to everyone :

Soonyam aakeernataam eti
Mrityurapyutsavaayate
Aapad-sampadivaabhaati
Vidvajjana-samaagame

Meaning: Be it a state of void, an occasion of death of a dear or near one, a situation of danger or calamity, if it is viewed and assimilated with enlightenment, in the presence of enlightened people, guided by them, it gets transformed into an inner festivity.

All the inequalities, imbalances and divergences are no doubt there in the world and people often complain about virtually everything around. But despite all these flagrant inequalities, the mind which is the real enjoyer or sufferer at every turn, is gifted with the unobliterable capacity to sublimate every outcome and interaction, so as to gain expansion and elevation every time.

Yes, such a positive note in thinking and attitude can be taken up, developed and preserved. I think Rakesh is striving to make this possible, and in the process inspiring and inducing his readers and friends to take to the same elevating path of life.

To have a public administrator in our midst live and reflect such positive notes of thinking and learning, and what more, to find him articulate in doing so, is greatly fulfilling. For any administrator, to be truly representing the country's heritage and ideals, this should be an inevitable quality and virtue.

Blessings

It is equally encouraging to find that another Public Administrator, retired from his service, puts his stamp of approval and confirmation to what Rakesh (his erstwhile student) has done. Every good teacher imparts his learning to the student only to enrich and empower him as much as possible. And if this role is rightly fulfilled, the student will become equally or more resourceful so as to impart the learning to others too. Only then the teacher's efforts bring fruition fully. The test of any good teaching is its ability to make the student a better teacher.

Well, such is the peerless tradition and culture of our land. And I am happy to note that this finds an encouraging illustration in the case of Rajeshwar Prasad and Rakesh Mittal.

I wish them all enrichment, elevation and fulfilment in life.

— Swami Bhoomananda Tirth

Narayanasrama Thapovanam
Trichur, Kerala.
28 August, 1995

Self-knowledge verily means freedom from the mind's shackles. Such freedom inevitably leads to inner composure, spiritual brilliance, and expansion of the heart and mind. When the seeker begins to revel in his inner delight, his mind's narrowness will give place to all fold love and oneness. The enlightened hearts thus become sarva-bhota-hite-rattah engaged in the welfare of all beings.

— Swamiji

CONTENTS

Foreword	vii
Preface	ix
Blessings	xi
1. Why to be Good	1
2. Integrity is a State of Mind	6
3. Learn to Trust	9
4. When Bad Things Happen to Good People	13
5. There is Enough Time	17
6. There is Enough Money	24
7. Progress in Z Direction	28
8. When You Don't Agree	30
9. Create Your Own Good World	32
10. We Get What We Wish	34
11. Small is Beautiful	36
12. We All are Coolies	41
13. Plan Your Landing	43
14. Think Positive	45
15. Keep the Strings Loose	49
16. Riding the World	52
17. Refuse to be Poor	56
18. Are You OK?	60
19. Secularism and National Development	63
20. No Need of Anger	73
21. When You lose	77

22.	Be Fair to God	80
23.	Life is a Game of Tennis	84
24.	Tip of the Iceberg	88
25.	Refuse to be Insulted	91
26.	Swami Chinmayananda in My Life	94
27.	The Heat is within Us	98
28.	Happy New Year	100
29.	Spiritual Investment	103
30.	We do not Need a Gun	106
31.	The Ganges does not Hoard	110
32.	How Lucky We are	112
33.	Brakes of Life Vehicle	115
34.	Whom do We Address to?	118
35.	Life and the Rubik Cube	121
36.	Refuse to Dislike	123
37.	Why should You Quit ?	126
38.	When Tears Turn the Life	129
39.	Peace at Any Price is Cheap	131
40.	Be Dangerously Honest	134
41.	The Wealth of Nature	137
42.	Living Perfectly	140
43.	When You Grow Wise	142
44.	Countdown for Launching	145
45.	Ganga or Sagar	148
46.	Life is a Process of Weeding	151
47.	I Have No Enemy	154
48.	Leading a Simple Life	157
49.	When You Miss Your Wish	160
50.	Conflict of a Sarovar	163
	The Mission Song	

1
WHY TO BE GOOD

Today, the life of man has become so complicated that he has lost sight of its primary goal. In this confusion, he has started believing that there is no point in being good and that good people are generally unsuccessful and unhappy. I got the inspiration to think over this matter quite some time back. At that time I was posted in a sensitive post. On my transfer from there, during a farewell dinner at a friend's place, a common friend of ours showed his concern by saying that I had worked very hard and honestly on that job but such persons generally regret in the end. I was taken aback by his remark and did not know what to say. Perhaps I was not in a position to say anything. Otherwise also I had never thought on this subject. What he said was perhaps the common viewpoint and he could not be blamed for that. At that time I only said that it was better to be dishonest than to regret being honest.

However, I was not satisfied and started thinking as to why one should be good. Was there any science of goodness? I have been a student of science and do not accept anything illogical. Hence I needed proper explanation of the same. During this search I came across some spiritual books which have been written very scientifically. In fact, I got the correct definition of 'religion' from these books as well as the answer to my query. Not that every doubt got removed immediately but the fundamentals became clear. The doubts which arose in course of time were also removed as a result of study and experience. Today, I can say with full conviction that it is fortunate to be a good person and in all situations goodness is strength and not weakness. However, it needs discussion as to how one should face today's society so that his goodness brings him respect instead of making him a laughing stock. In this write-up we shall discuss the same.

First of all, one should know the meaning of 'goodness'. Generally the mistake is committed here itself. In all parts of the world one religion or the other is followed. After all, why did we need religion ? As mankind developed and formed society, the need for a set of rules of life was felt. Religion was the result of this need. In a way mankind got religion in the form of 'Constitution of Life'. With the change in the circumstances, amendments were required in this constitution and as a result new religions came into being. However, there are certain cardinal principles which are same in all religions. We may call them fundamental principles of life. There can hardly be any difference of opinion on these principles. In my view to follow these fundamental principles of life is 'goodness'. This way goodness is a social need more than an individual need. It is necessary not only for individual happiness but for social happiness too. Unfortunately, this faith is getting eroded while no alternative is suggested for social as well as individual happiness. As a result, man today is in such a dilemma where he does not know how to achieve happiness. By the time he realises that happiness lies in following the path of goodness only, generally it is too late.

To establish a relationship between 'goodness' and 'happiness' it would be necessary to contemplate upon certain points. Though one may take a very philosophical view on the subject, we shall confine ourselves to its practical aspect only in this discussion. The first question which comes to everyone's mind is "what is the goal of human life?" The most realistic answer to this would be that 'attainment of happiness' is the goal of human life. The next question arises, 'what is happiness?' There can be several answers to this question and it will depend upon the intellectual development and experience of an individual. Therefore, it needs some explanation so that some sort of consensus may be brought on the definition of happiness.

I would only like to say there is no definite relationship between material prosperity and happiness. It cannot be said with certainty that a materially prosperous man is always happy or vice versa. For example, wealth may be a cause of happiness but it can equally be a cause of misery. A son may be a cause of happiness but he can equally be a cause of misery. A high position may be a cause of happiness but it can equally be cause of misery. We can give several such examples. These examples are not merely for the sake of argument but these are the facts of life which no one can deny. Thus there should not be any doubt that happiness is a state of mind and the goal of human life is to achieve that state of mind.

Now the question is how to achieve such state of mind and if there is any way, following which one can achieve such state of mind, it is advisable to follow that path only. If we take this criteria as a touchstone, the dilemma of life will disappear. However, it is necessary to be honest while judging ourselves on this touchstone and there should be no cleverness. If we do so, we shall deceive none but ourselves. It can be said with certainty that anything which does not fall in the category of goodness will fail on this touchstone. If we want to achieve the mental state of happiness, there is no option but to follow goodness. This way, by being good, we favour none but ourselves. For example, if we do not carry a feeling of revenge, we get more benefited than anyone else. Similarly, if we follow truth, we are the first beneficiary. Several such examples can be given. On the other hand the path of evil can never lead to that state of mind which we are seeking. This can also be confirmed by several examples.

From the above, it appears that if happiness is achieved so easily by following the path of goodness, why does everyone not follow the same ? Essentially, the nature of man is this only but it is not easy to discriminate between the path of goodness and the path of evil. Everyone feels that what he is doing will lead to happiness. Only a fortunate few are able to look and think beyond their immediate surroundings. Generally, the path of evil is more attractive in the beginning than the path of goodness. Due to this attraction one starts following the same. He also finds this path to be more crowded which removes his doubt. Once on the path of evil, he tends to remain there either due to ignorance or, perhaps, it is too late to change the course. While he knows his mistake, he does not admit it. Not only this, he discourages others too from following the path of goodness by giving them a false image of his happiness. As a result those who want to follow the righteous path either do not follow it at all or leave the same midstream. Then they also start advocating against the path of goodness. The suggestion given by my friend in the beginning is applicable to such persons who give up the path of goodness in the mid-course. Those who complete their journey on this path cannot even think of regretting it.

In the end it is necessary to contemplate upon how to face today's world while being on the righteous path. I will mention here a line from the book *The Inner Reality* by Paul Braunton. While discussing the similar situation he has said, "Be ye harmless like a dove, but wise as serpent". This clarifies the whole approach. While it is necessary not to harm others, it is also necessary not to get harmed as a result of our goodness. However, it should be clearly understood whether the situation which we take as harmful is in reality so or not and whether it adversely affects us and the society. If yes, we should oppose it with firmness and establish that the righteous path is our strength and not weakness. This kind of firmness is very essential in today's world. It should also be kept in mind that a person on the path of evil is a weak person and normally our firmness is enough to beat him. But if our goodness gives an impression of weakness the fault lies with us and we have to remove this fault by proper introspection.

Thus it is proved that in order to achieve the goal of life, there is no alternative but to follow the righteous path. In the short run, the goal may not be visible but it is finally achieved on this path only. This is an eternal truth like any scientific principle.

❋

- Be not merely good, be good for something.
- Disease and misfortune come to do us good in the long run.
- Goodness does not brook a thought of return.
- Goodness is always an asset. A man who is straight, friendly and useful may never be famous, but he is respected and liked by all who know him.
- It is only by doing good to others that one attains one's own good.
- There can be no good so long as malice and jealousy prevail.
- We can do more good by being good than in any other way.
- What is good for others may not be good for you.

2
INTEGRITY IS A STATE OF MIND

Today, Integrity is a much talked about word, particularly in public life. All public servants are supposed to have integrity beyond doubt. A certificate is also supposed to be given to every civil servant about his integrity. And most of them get the certificates. But can we say that the integrity of civil servants in general is beyond doubt or even satisfactory for the matter ? If not, it has to be deeply analysed. We shall dwell upon this subject in this article.

Before we do so, the word 'Integrity' should itself be properly understood. The normal meaning given to this word is 'Not Taking Bribe'. The *Chambers Dictionary* meaning of this word is — Entireness; Wholeness; The unimpaired state of anything; Uprightness; Honesty; Purity. Obviously 'Integrity' is a much wider term than what is normally understood.

A public servant, while discharging his duties, is supposed to have a complete view of the situation without being influenced by external factors and take upright decision with pure and honest mind. This is what can be an ideal definition of the quality called 'Integrity'. Therefore, any deviation from this would mean loss of integrity. 'Bribe' is one factor, though a prominent one, which is likely to cause deviation. But other factors also cause deviation. These may be fear of survival, caste consideration, prejudice, vendetta, suspicion, over-ambition, etc. Deviation from correct decision due to any of these factors also means loss of integrity. Then there are factors like misuse of power, wastage of resources, etc., which are generally overlooked. My personal view is that such loss of integrity is causing more harm to the system than mere acceptance of bribes. Therefore, there is need for suitable checks in these areas also.

Unfortunately, our system has miserably failed to check this evil despite many administrative measures. This is mainly because 'Integrity' is basically a 'State of Mind' which cannot be influenced much only by administrative measures. It is a sum total of the influences of various factors and in a way reflects the state of the society. There can always be found a counter to any administrative measure. Such measures will be effective only when there is influence at the mental level also. Otherwise, those who have already deviated will keep on deviating more and more while the administrative measures will remain in force for those who do not need them.

Therefore, the role of those in superior positions in all walks of life (not merely public services) becomes important. Indian people, by and large are a satisfied lot and happily accept their condition provided the leaders of the society show their integrity. Unfortunately, it has not been the case and the result is obvious. The old principle that one should not only be clean but also appear clean has been grossly misused. The entire emphasis has shifted to appearing clean rather than being clean. Many do not care even to appear clean. Very obvious corruption charges are refuted by responsible persons on the ground that the charges are not proved. Many times they don't even care to say that charges are wrong. And all of us know how difficult it is to prove such charges. In such a state of affairs, it is no use blaming lesser mortals and apply administrative measures to them. In fact, those who are supposed to apply these measures are themselves not above board. Thus the exercise becomes all the more futile.

There is need of establishing that corruption ultimately leads to unhappiness in the society at large. To begin with, some people may feel happy at the cost of others but a stage comes when everyone becomes a victim of the system. In the present age of science and technology this will have to be established in a logical manner. All people may not understand the science of our scriptures which pleads for right conduct. There have to be economic and social explanations of the havocs, the corruption plays with the society. It should establish that if we do not mend our ways, the whole society will have to pay the price.

Fortunately, the roots of our society are deep and strong. So far the damage of our values can be said to be only surface damage. The people of India, by and large, are God-fearing satisfied lot. At the same time they are aware of their strength. Those in high places should not take them for granted. If they do not mend their ways gracefully, people will force them to do so. This is where the hope lies. Let us hope that all those in responsible positions will work with full 'integrity' not by compulsion but by choice. The rest of the society will automatically follow them. In that event administrative measures can also be taken effectively against the defaulters.

- A man of integrity is accepted, believed, trusted and befriended by all.
- A man of integrity will never listen to any plea against conscience.
- Integrity has no need for rules.
- Integrity is self-rewarding.
- Honesty is still the best policy with a little bit of commonsense.
- An honest man is the noblest work of God.
- It pays to be honest, but it's slow pay.

3
LEARN TO TRUST

The management-employee relationship is very important for the progress of an organisation. 'Man' is the most important resource of any organisation but perhaps least attention is paid towards man-making. We always pay more attention towards resources like building, equipments, furniture, etc. The management may sometimes be unduly concerned about working hours also. It is not that these areas are not important. They certainly are, but in my view these are subservient to man, who is the core of the organisation. Unless there is an inner urge to work, no amount of external facilities can motivate a man to improve his productivity. They can at best help marginally.

Now the question arises as to how an inner urge can be created in human beings. I must hasten to add here that an inner urge is something which is always there. It may be dormant in some persons. The meaning of creation is to revive this urge. Human beings are basically divine and this fact is to be accepted before making efforts in developing them. The approach should therefore be to trust your men. Someone may say that trusting may at times be harmful. To this I will only say that non-trusting is always harmful, while trusting is occasionally so. By trusting, an organisation always stands to gain. Of course, trusting does not at all mean 'not being careful'. That one has always to be. Even while one walks on the road, one has to be careful. This does not mean that one should not walk on the road.

Trusting is a two-way process but the initiative has to come from those in superior position. A precondition of trust is the realisation of a common objective. The goal of an organisation should be well defined and known to everyone. An individual should also know his role in the realisation of the goal and feel proud of it. A feeling should prevail in the organisation that everyone is important at his place and should be treated with dignity. The dignity of the lowest paid employee is as important as that of the chief executive or perhaps even more than him.

Having created such an atmosphere in the organisation, one can safely trust his colleagues. The general experience as well as my personal experience have shown that more than eighty per cent of the employees do respond positively. Others should be given the benefit of doubt. The management should think from their point of view. May be their past experiences have not been good. May be their personal life is not happy or maybe the management has not done justice in some of their personal matters. And lastly, some margin for the circumstances around may also be given. Once these factors have been taken care of, another ten per cent follow the suit and fall in the mainstream of the organisation.

The remaining ten per cent or less may not be fortunate enough to understand this philosophy. We need not be unduly concerned about them. The only factor which should be kept in mind while dealing with them is an open approach. The management should be careful of not getting biased towards them but should deal with them on merit. This includes firm action whenever necessary. My experience is that such occasions arise rarely. The force of ninety per cent will be strong enough to deal with these ten per cent.

This process should be continued, otherwise there may be cracks in course of time. Communication is something very important for this. In the absence of proper communication, even good intentions of management or employees are misunderstood and lead to unhealthy situations. My personal view is that there should be minimum secrecy in decision making. Once we accept the principle of participative management, I do not see any reason why decisions should be secret. It may be so in rare cases. It is my firm belief that secrecy is an indication of weakness. The greater the secrecy of decision, for whatsoever reasons, the greater are the chances of rifts between the management and employees. Therefore, it is necessary to create forums where communication may take place in a healthy atmosphere. This may be in the form of joint councils, quality circles or periodical meetings.

After communication-comes the timely decision on personal matters. Mere good intentions are not enough unless these are converted into action. Small matters in the view of management like annual increments, crossing of efficiency bars, GPF advance, leave sanction, T.A. bill sanction etc., are very important from an individual's point of view. A system should be developed so that these problems are taken care of before any need of complaint arises. I have come across several cases where there has been criminal neglect in the disposal of such matters. No wonder, the affected employees had lost all their initiative.

Another important factor is the working environment. It should be ensured that your men's working environment is reasonably good, keeping in view the resources of the organisation. I am of the view that lavish expenditure is not necessary for this purpose. All that is needed is to take timely care of the furniture and other equipments. The management should not expect good work from a person who sits on a broken chair. I also feel that the management should not incur unnecessary expenditure for the senior officers and there should be minimum gap between management and employees' working environment. Once these attitudes are developed, it becomes easy to develop a proper work culture.

And then there is need to keep your employees as up-to-date as possible. The management gets several opportunities of interaction with the outer world and thus remains aware of the developments but the staff does not get such opportunities. While equal opportunities may not be possible, their knowledge should be updated through training, seminars or other forums of discussions. My experience in this area has been very positive. This is liked by most of the staff and they respond wonderfully if the job is done seriously.

I will not touch upon other areas which make an organisation conducive to growth. The intention here was to highlight the 'Man' part of the organisation which I feel is the most important resource of all the four 'M's, namely, Man, Money, Material and Moments. And to develop 'Man' we must 'LEARN TO TRUST'.

- God can make you anything you want to be. The secret is 'Trust Him'.
- It is an equal failing to trust everybody and to trust nobody.
- The man who trusts men will make fewer mistakes than he who distrusts them.
- The only way to make a man trustworthy is to trust him.
- To be trusted is a greater compliment than to be loved.
- Trust is like a thin thread. Once you break it, it is almost impossible to put it together again.
- Trusting is occasionally painful. Not trusting is always so.
- What upsets me is not that you lied to me but that from now onwards I can no longer trust you.

4
WHEN BAD THINGS HAPPEN TO GOOD PEOPLE

During my U.K. visit in 1990, I came across a wonderful book titled *'When Bad Things Happen to Good People'*. I reached London on 27 April and on the 29, visited my niece. She is a very positive and helpful person. At that time a relation of hers (a young lady) was staying there and had come for a knee operation. There was problem in one of her knees and it was to be operated upon. It was a major operation scheduled for 14 May.

We were all talking about this. I found the lady to be confident and positive. It pleased us all and then we started talking about 'Why Bad Things Happen to Good People'. The lady was a lecturer in a reputed public school of Delhi. She had been a good player all through her student life. So much so, she aimed to join IPS, which she could not do for various reasons. She got married to a well placed man working for an international airline. She had a son and they were leading a happy and successful life. And suddenly the trouble came. By no stretch of imagination, they could think of this development. After the operation, perhaps, she was not to be her normal self and she knew it well. But she was still positive in her attitude and confidently participated in the discussion.

As we were trying to draw our conclusions about such happenings, the husband of my niece took out the book *When Bad Things Happen to Good People* written by Harold S Kushner. The book was obviously most relevant to our subject of discussion. I was told that it was a rare book and not easily available. Since I was to stay in the U.K. for about three months, I borrowed the book and went through it immediately thereafter. And it turned out to be a wonderful book. Then the thought came to my mind to prepare a write-up on the conclusions of the book and present it to my friends. I am sure that this thoughtful, life-affirming book will help you cope with hard times and personal pain. Filled with compassion, it will give you comfort and strength when tragedy threatens to take away your faith and help you understand that God can fulfil the deepest needs of an anguished heart.

The author is a rabbi of Jews (clergyman) in the USA. When he was young, he had a son who was a bright and happy child. The family was a very happy one but suddenly the child was detected for a very strange disease. His hair started falling out after he turned one-year-old and stopped growing. Doctors called this phenomenon 'Progeria'. They told the author that the child would never grow beyond three feet in height, would have no hair on his head or body, would look like a little old man while he was still a child and would die in his early teens.

How does one handle news like that ? Like any other common man, the author felt deeply shocked and questioned God's fairness. He was a good man doing all that a good person is supposed to do. The question 'Why did it happen to him only ?' came to his mind again and again. He started searching for answers to it and the book is result of that search. The boy, of course, died at the age of fourteen as predicted but the thinking of the author reduced the agony of the reality to a great extent and changed his life altogether in the time to come.

The misfortune of good people are not only a problem to the people who suffer and their families, they are a problem for everyone who wants to believe in a just and fair and livable world. They inevitably raise questions about the goodness, the kindness and even the existence of God. The general attitude is the assumption that we get what we deserve and we always try to find reasons for justifying whatever happens to us. At times we also try to establish that the tragedy has happened for our good.

While there is no harm in taking this line of thought, the problem with this reasoning is that it does not really help the sufferer or explain his suffering. It is primarily to defend God, to use words and ideas to transform bad into good and pain into privilege. In a way, we also try to establish that God is the cause of our suffering and also make ourselves feel guilty in addition to the burden of tragedy.

The author has taken altogether different view of the situation. He cannot imagine of a God who can be cruel at any time. He has tried to establish that life consists of good and bad things. And happening of bad things is as much a matter of chance, as those of good things in anybody's life. God does not want bad things to happen but perhaps it is not in His hands. He also does not want bad things to happen as much as we want. Some are caused by bad luck, some are caused by bad people and some are simply an inevitable consequence of our being human and being mortal, living in a world of inflexible natural laws. The painful things that happen to us are not punishment for our misbehaviour, nor are they in any way part of some grand design on God's part. Because the tragedy is not God's will, we need not feel hurt or betrayed by God when tragedy strikes. Instead, we can turn to Him for help in overcoming it because God is as outraged by the tragedy as we are.

And this is how bad things have a meaning in the lives of good people. It turns them to God all the more. That is to say, that bad things that happen to us in our lives do not have a meaning when they happen to us. They do not happen for any good reason which would cause us to accept them willingly. But we can give meaning to them. We can redeem these tragedies from senselessness by imposing meaning upon them. The question we should be asking is not 'Why did this happen to me?' 'What did I do to deserve this?' That is really an unanswerable, pointless question. A better question would be 'Now that this has happened to me, what am I going to do about it ?'

And this is where God comes to our help in the form of a good friend, a good relative, a good idea or courage. God inspires some people to help others who have been hurt by life. God makes them want to become doctors and nurses, to spend days and nights of self-sacrificing concern with an intensity for which no money can compensate, in an effort to sustain life and alleviate pain. And this concern, courage, in due course gives a meaning to the tragedy.

In the end, the author concludes that his own tragedy had a great meaning. He believes that his son served God's purpose not by being sick or strange-looking (there was no reason why God should have wanted that), but by facing up so bravely to his illness and to the problems caused by his appearance. His friends and schoolmates were affected by his courage and by the way he managed to live a full life despite his limitations. The people who knew his family were moved to handle the difficult times in their own lives with greater hope and courage when they saw this example.

None of us can avoid the problem of why bad things happen to good people. The question is 'Are we capable of forgiving and loving the people around us, even if they have hurt us and let us down by not being perfect. Can we forgive and love God even when we have found out that He is not perfect, even when He has let us down and disappointed us by permitting bad luck and sickness and cruelty in His world, and permitting some of these things to happen to us ?'

And if we can do these things, we shall be able to recognise that the ability to forgive and to love are the weapons God has given us to enable us to live fully, bravely and meaningfully in this less-than-perfect world. The question 'Why bad things happen to good people' will then lose its significance.

- Adversity causes some men to break, others to break records.
- Adversity introduces a man to himself.
- Adversity is afraid of one who is not afraid of adversity.
- Adversity makes man wise but not rich.
- A winner gets scars too.

5
THERE IS ENOUGH TIME

I have not attended even a single function at which the chief guest was not a very busy person and not in a hurry to leave. So is the case with most of the so-called important persons. They are always busy and have no time even to think as to why are they so busy. One also wonders if most of the important persons of the society are so busy, the shape of things in all the spheres should have been excellent. But is that so? If not, then of what use is their busyness?

I have pondered a great deal over this subject and am of the view that most of us waste a lot of time though we always appear to be very busy. I also hold that there is enough time for everything which falls within official or social duty. And I take duty in a much wider sense. It is only a question of making optimum use of our time by planning it well. I will even go to the extent of saying that the day can be of more than twenty-four hours for a well planned person and I mean it. I also believe that a busy man has more time than a free man. So efforts should be made to remain busy but in a productive and healthy manner.

All my above thinking was confirmed by a book on time management by M R Pai. I am mentioning about the book because I could go through it on account of my time planning. Once I was returning from Bombay. After reaching the airport I learnt that the flight was late by four hours. (Ultimately it was delayed by ten hours.) I had the option either to go back to the city or to wait at the airport itself. Since there was no worthwhile assignment in mind for the city, I decided to wait at the airport itself and also sent back the manager who had come to see me off. At the airport I visited the bookshop and came across some good books. I bought some including the above mentioned one. Thus I could not only go through the books, but also the waiting became a pleasure, and instead of cursing Indian Airlines, I felt grateful towards it. Since the book was small and reasonably priced, I bought few more copies of it for some of my friends and it was appreciated by all who read it. I, therefore, thought it proper to share the contents (which are confirmed by my own personal experience) with more of my friends.

First of all we must believe in the value of time and consider it as a very important resource. We generally talk of three resources, namely MAN, MONEY and MATERIAL. Add the fourth resource to it: MOMENTS. This resource differs from others in a vital respect. Once it is lost it cannot be replaced. If money is lost, it can be borrowed, if material is lost, fresh stocks can be built up; if trained staff leave, new staff can be recruited. But if time is lost, it cannot be regained or replaced. For time management, it is essential to develop this consciousness of the value of time as a resource.

The next step is time-budgeting. More than money, time is to be budgeted properly. First draw up an annual plan with regard to all important business and personal items. Every quarter, draw up a fairly detailed plan for the quarter. Every month end, draw up a plan for the following month and so with the week. Every day, in the morning, plan in detail the day's activities. Time spent in all this planning will be rewarded in the form of better efficiency. Various models can be drawn up for a daily time budget and one can choose according to one's convenience.

The approach to time management should be an integrated one. It has to take into account all aspects of your daily life. However, for purpose of discussion, time can be divided into three aspects-biological time, business or office Time and social time. The general principles of these aspects shall be discussed here in order to make best use of time.

BIOLOGICAL TIME

Your body is the instrument of work and should be kept in very good order. Biological needs like sleep, food and recreation should, therefore, be well regulated. Time management with regard to these biological needs, therefore, assumes great significance. There are four general principles of biological time management:

a) *Treat all days alike.* Treating some days as holidays and some others as working days upsets the routine. If you get up at the same time and complete ablution and other daily necessities, you will get a complete grip on the activities of the entire day.

b) *In all repetitive activities.* Find out time-saving efficiency techniques. For instance, even if you save five minutes every day in bathing or shaving, you will have saved thirty hours in a year.

c) *Regulate your daily activities in a clock-like fashion.* It means that, by and large, there should be a fixed time for your biological activities like food, exercise, sleep, etc.

d) *It is advisable to develop the habit of getting up early in the morning. It has several advantages.* The mind is fresh and powerful. There are no disturbances. The environment is quiet and you can work with tremendous concentration. However, those who cannot get up early should develop the habit of staying awake late at night. But it is certain that two hours of early morning are much more than two hours of late night in terms of efficiency.

BUSINESS TIME

Time spent in office or at business place is known as business time and is obviously very important. There are some general principles governing business time. They are:

a) Feel healthy and cheerful when you are in office or at business place. If you don't feel so, it may be advisable to stay home and take rest. Your irritation in office may cost very dearly.

b) Reach your workplace well in time and, if possible, little before time. This changes the whole atmosphere of the office and in all likelihood you will be able to leave office in time in the evening also. The day's output of the whole office will also increase tremendously.

c) Structure your office time suitably depending upon your needs. However, the structure should be able to take care of unforeseen situations. This is necessary to avoid irritation when such situations appear.

d) Make the best use of your support services like telephone, intercom, fax machine, personal staff, etc. Be judicious in deciding the job you should do yourself. Try to delegate as much as possible.

e) Be precise and clear in your communication be it verbal or written. Instructions to your subordinates should be very clear, otherwise at the end of the day everybody's effort may go waste.

f) Keep your table tidy and encourage everyone to do the same. The papers and files should be well arranged. This saves a lot of time.

g) Be brief and businesslike while meeting visitors. Those who unnecessarily prolong discussion should be firmly told not to do so. Avoid offering tea or coffee to visitors, and if it has to be offered, make sure that it is served in the least possible time.

h) Advise important visitors to seek prior appointment as far as possible. The same practice should be followed when you go to meet others.

i) Plan your tours wisely and try to cover as many assignments as are conveniently possible in one visit. Keep addresses and telephone numbers properly recorded in your diary, and it should be readily available.

j) Attend promptly to small matters like submitting T A bills, verifying your GPF account, sending replies to various letters which cannot be passed on to the office, etc. A reminder will only add to your work. You are likely to take more time in recollecting the facts, once reply is delayed.

k) If you attend a meeting, try to find when your presence is required and be present accordingly. In case it is not possible to do so take some paper or file which may be gone through, if your participation in the meeting is not required for some length of time.

1) And lastly, believe that others' time is as important as that of yours. Never waste others' time for lack of planning. Ultimately it is the output of the whole organisation which matters and not merely yours.

These are some of the principles which should be followed in order to make best use of business time. The list is not exhaustive and many more points can be added. But the scope of managing business time much more efficiently is well established.

Social Time

Social time is the time you give to your own development, to your family and friends and for social activities. Many businessmen and executives feel that their business obligations are so heavy that they cannot find sufficient time for their family. Their thinking is totally wrong and counter-productive. Such people end up by paying a heavy price for their so-called busy schedule. Proper management of social time is as important as the other two aspects of time. Some important aspects of social time Management are given below :

a) All family members should meet at least once every day and exchange information and views. This promotes close family bonds and lays the foundation for a happy and successful life.

b) At least one morning in a week should also be reserved for the family. And, once or twice a year all should go out of town for a brief holiday.

c) Some people develop a habit of carrying office files to their homes. As far as possible, this should be avoided.

d) Paying social visits and attending parties are unavoidable, but too much of them can destroy your private life. So carefully choose the occasions, which should be attended. You should also develop the art of saying 'no' if you find it difficult to attend some occasion. Writing a good letter or giving a courteous phone call is most practical way of doing so.

e) For every visit, lay down an average time limit. Once people come to know that you do not waste any time, and even when you visit them you spend only half an hour or an hour utmost, they will respect your sense of time.

f) Social visits should be preceded by some intimation. Unscheduled visits always take a longer time than preplanned ones.
g) You must have time every day for thinking. The greater your responsibility, the more time you need for thinking. Early morning walks can be a good time to think. This time should not at all be wasted in gossiping.
h) Waiting at places like airport, railway or bus station can be used for thinking or reading. Travelling also provides an excellent opportunity for thinking and reading.
i) Reading is an important aspect of social time. If you analyse your reading material you will find that it falls into the following categories:
   1. Daily newspapers, magazine or current affairs,
   2. Professional magazines,
   3. Professional books,
   4. General books and,
   5. Classics.

The first principle is to be selective in your reading; the second is to plan your reading. For instance, do not buy 15 or 20 magazines. Select the essential ones and go through them properly. As regards books, you should make a realistic list of books to be read every year. Such a list should also provide a room for any new book which should be read immediately. Some part of reading time should be reserved for professional magazines and latest books on your subject so that you are always up-to-date in your line of work.

Reading the daily newspaper is not only a habit but also a necessity. However, one should be selective here also. There is no point in going through too many newspapers. The choice should be limited to two or three papers. One should also develop the habit of reading them rapidly and meaningfully.

j) Apart from these personal needs, one should find some time for social activities also. This will depend upon the individual's liking. But it should be carefully selected and the contribution should be meaningful. It should not merely for the sake of it,

There Is Enough Time

otherwise, it may be counter-productive. One can serve the society through such activities and derive satisfaction. A well planned man can easily find time for such activities also.

Thus we have covered all the aspects of time management. It may not be possible to follow all of them at once but as one proceeds in this direction, they will automatically be followed. And then you will also end up saying, "THERE IS ENOUGH TIME".

- A good secret of how best to use each day's time is to try to pack it like a suitcase, filling up the small spaces with small things.
- As every thread of gold is valuable, so is every moment of time.
- Doing the duty of the time is the best way to live.
- Everything has its time. The desire to reach things before the right time means overreaching them.
- Manage your time as you manage your money.
- Short as life is, we make it still shorter by the careless waste of time.
- There is enough time. Don't waste time in thinking that it is not enough.
- Time is the same for all of us; the diligent catches hold of it; the foolish lets it pass.
- Time misspent is not lived but lost.
- Well arranged time is the surest mark of a well arranged mind.
- You can work forty-eight hours a day if you plan well.

6
THERE IS ENOUGH MONEY

These days rarely do we find a person who is happy within his income. It is true that prices have been going up at a fast rate but so have incomes. I don't mean to say that prices have not adversely affected the common man. But I definitely do not consider this the only reason for being unhappy with what most of us get. I believe that in most of the cases 'there is enough money' and it depends on us how wisely we use it without sacrificing the essential needs of life. This is what we shall try to establish in this article.

Swami Chinmayanandji, in his book *'Kindle Life'*, has described the 'Happiness Index' as the ratio of number of desires fulfilled divided by the number of desires entertained. That is:

$$\text{Happiness Index} = \frac{\text{No. of desires fulfilled}}{\text{No. of desires entertained}}$$

There can be two ways of raising this index, i.e., by increasing the numerator or by decreasing the denominator. The trouble with most of us is that as the number of desires fulfilled increases, the number of desires entertained also increases at much faster rate. This results in the fall of the value of the 'Happiness Index'. With this kind of approach it will never be possible to raise the Happiness Index, no matter what may be the increase in our incomes or resources. So if the index is to be raised, at least the denominator should remain constant. The better way of raising the index would be to decrease the number of desires entertained, once our essential needs are fulfilled. And the index will become infinite, if the number of desires is reduced to zero. That is to say that a desireless or wantless person is the happiest person. We, however, have no intention of advocating such a state of mind.

This analysis brings us to the conclusion that if we want to be happy within our means, we have to reduce our needs and desires. To do so we shall have to rationally analyse our present needs with an open mind. And if we do so I am sure that there will be many areas in which money can be saved without discomfort. Broadly the needs or desires can be classified into three categories:

1. Essential needs.
2. Comfort needs.
3. Luxury needs.

Fulfilment of essential needs is necessary for survival. Food, clothing, shelter, education and health-care fall in this category. Among these, food is the most important. One need not give many arguments to establish that there can be wide range of expenditure on all these essential needs. However, one should believe in the basic fact that the nature has given us enough for our needs but not for our greed. That being so, it depends upon us as to how we spend on these essential needs. For example, when we talk of food, the main criteria should be the nutrition and we all know that nutritious food is not necessarily costly. In all probability it will be other way round. For example, seasonal and fresh fruits/vegetables are generally the cheapest and most nutritious. All food items if properly planned in terms of requirements and timings can save a lot of money. The same is the case with clothing. Here the main criteria should be the decency and convenience. Costly dresses are not always decent. Also maintaining more than reasonable number of dresses is not only expensive but also inconvenient. One can easily establish norms of adding new dresses and at the same time helping the poor people by giving them the old dresses.

As far as shelter is concerned, it is more difficult to draw a line. At the same time it is one of the major items of expenditure. Unfortunately, in our country, the concept of constructing functional houses is missing and in most of the cases money is spent for the sake of spending. There is vast scope for saving money in the construction of houses without sacrificing comfort, nay, with more comfort. It is mainly because of the extravagance of those who have excessive money, that the construction of house is becoming more and more difficult for the common man. Well, that being a bigger issue, those who construct houses with limited resources should try to be as functional as possible. The main criteria should be proper light, ventilation and safety. Those who go for rented houses should also look for these features. A small, well-kept house is always better appreciated than an ill-kept big one.

Similar planning is required in the field of education and health care. These also vary widely in terms of quality and cost. Expenditure on education can be saved by proper selection of school, proper attention on children and efficient use of aids. In case of health care, the attention should be more on prevention than cure. These days there is too much emphasis on costly medicines. It may not always be possible to avoid them but most of the time one can manage with economic treatment.

Having met the essential needs one should properly plan the needs falling in the category of comfort. Items like television, refrigerator, means of transport, etc., may be said to fall in this category for most of the middle-class families. There is more scope for showing wisdom in this area and one should understand his limitations well. In no case should one stretch these needs beyond his means.

The last category of needs is luxury needs. These may be called 'desires', and 'happiness index' mainly depends upon them. One desire generally leads to another and there is no end to them. Hence, there is need to be careful right in the beginning, otherwise one ends up losing not only money but mental peace too. Therefore, luxury needs should always be given up. In all probability 'desires' take away one's happiness, in the long run, if not immediately. The interesting thing is that individually most of us feel that extravagance is bad but somehow we keep on indulging in it. Therefore, need is to get away from this cycle. The so-called society (which is perhaps we are afraid of) consists of individuals and if they feel otherwise, where is the question of society not appreciating it? But someone has to make the beginning. Why not we?

A good technique to plan expenditure is to ask two questions whenever a need is felt in mind. One, whether it is essential, and if it is not, drop it then and there. In case it turns out to be essential, the next question should be whether it can be postponed. If yes, it should be postponed. Most likely it will become non-essential during the period of postponement. If even after that it remains essential and immediate, it should be fulfilled. Also frequent visits to market should be avoided. Many non-essential needs become essential when you go around the market. As far as possible one should go to the market with a definite list of items on paper or in mind and confine his purchases to that.

Thus, if a man keeps control over his desires and wisely spends his resources on essential personal and social needs, there will be no occasion for complaining. And if society at large is able to do so even the bad shape of the economy, which we see today, will improve. And then most of us will start believing that "there is enough money".

- Hold your money merely as custodian for what is God's.
- If money does not bring happiness, give it back.
- Money is a good servant but a bad master.
- Money is not evil if in good hands.

7
PROGRESS IN Z DIRECTION

'Progress' is a much talked about subject. Progress is, and should be, the aim of everyone, be it at the individual level, group level or national level. In the present article we shall briefly discuss about the progress at the individual level, though the conclusion will be applicable at the collective level also since the individual progress automatically leads to collective progress.

The simplest meaning of the word 'progress' according to *Chamber's Dictionary* is 'forward movement'. It is silent over the direction of movement and forward is a relative term. Also the factor to be looked into is the 'Purpose of Progress'. Assuming that the purpose of progress is happiness at all levels, we shall try to analyse as to why so much misery exists despite 'progress' in all fields.

Now when we talk of the direction, let us assume a three-dimensional space consisting of X, Y and Z axes. Let us also assume that the earthly plane is the X Y plane and the Z axis be the vertical direction. The progress we generally talk about and try to achieve is at the X Y plane that is at the earthly level. This kind of progress can never result in universal happiness. It is practically impossible for all to move in the forward direction on the X Y plane, because there is not enough space. In economic terms there are not enough resources for all to develop equally on the material plane. Such a dream will never come true.

That being so, what is the option or the desired strategy? Here comes the Z axis. Unless movement is in the higher direction, the real progress will never be possible. And as one moves higher and higher, material progress starts appearing more and more insignificant. A comparable example can be that of flying in an aeroplane. As one goes higher up in the sky, the divisions of villages, towns, provinces and even countries keep going in the background. One really starts wondering as to why there are so many man-made barriers. If such becomes the thinking while one is at physically higher level for a short period, one can imagine the state of mind of a person who remains at a higher level of thinking all the time. That is to say, unless the parameters of progress change, its objective can never be achieved. And for that, one has to rise above the material plane. Here the question of lack of space (or resources) does not arise. From a higher level of thinking the differences at the materials plane will look very insignificant.

I don't mean to say that efforts to make progress at the XY Plane should not be made. But I definitely believe that mere progress at this plane does not achieve the objective of progress. For that, one has to progress in the Z direction. As long as we aim only at material progress, the result will be the same. For example, the world has been trying to remove poverty for a long time but are we not poorer than ever before? The people may be moving above, the poverty line moves up even at a faster pace. Therefore, we should plan progress not only in the X Y directions but also in the Z direction. We may call them worldly directions and the spiritual direction respectively. Then only the objective of 'progress' can be achieved.

> When the selfish side of our life dies away, the nobler, bigger, braver God-side will manifest itself.

8
WHEN YOU DON'T AGREE

Almost daily we come across situations with which we do not agree. It may be a situation at home, at office, at marketplace or anywhere else. For example, your son may not be doing as well as you expect him to do. The subordinate may not be as honest as you expect him to be. The shopkeeper's behaviour may not be as polite as it should be, so on and so forth. One is generally at a loss to understand what should be the attitude in such situations. We shall briefly discuss this in the present article.

There can be three ways of dealing with such situations. The first is to 'REACT'. It means that you immediately express your disagreement in explicit terms, often with anger. This is the worst way of dealing with the situation. In this way, while you lose your own peace of mind, you do no good to the person or situation with whom you don't agree. By reacting immediately you are likely to lose sight of the positive side of the person. As a result the chances of the other person making any amends become very feeble and the overall situation becomes from bad to worse. The experience is that when you realise your hurried reaction, you end up making more compromise with the situation than what you would have normally made. Also reaction is an indication of your own weakness and indicates lack of conviction in your thinking. A person who believes in and practises virtue has no need to react.

The second way of dealing with a situation with which you don't agree is to 'TOLERATE' it. This is superior to the first approach. In tolerating you do not express your disagreement externally but internally you do not accept the situation. Normally this affects you internally. While this may or may not have a positive effect on the situation or person which is troubling you, it definitely has a negative effect on you. To some extent it also indicates the presence of the ego in you because when you tolerate a situation or person, a certain amount of repulsion or hate is implied. It brings you down and there is a good probability of you losing mental peace.

The best way to deal with a situation with which you do not agree is to accept it. This may raise several doubts in your mind. The first is whether it would amount to escapism. This is not true provided you do your duty to improve the situation or the person. Many times you may not be in a position to take any effective step. In that case you can politely give your advice without expecting compliance. It will generally go into the subconscious mind of the person responsible for the situation. This way you improve the chances of changing the person or the situation without losing your mental peace.

Unfortunately, what most of us do is to change ourselves on the lines of wrong persons or situations and then justify our slips. But does it really help anyone? No one, and not you in the least. The ultimate aim of everyone is mental peace and happiness and it cannot be achieved when you 'react' or 'tolerate'. Only 'acceptance', of having done your duty, is the right option.

- A wise man is one who can live in peace with things he cannot change.
- When we have accepted the worst, we have nothing more to lose. Result is true peace of mind.
- Accept what you cannot change.

9
CREATE YOUR OWN GOOD WORLD

The world we live in is very bad. This is what most of us have come to believe. Somehow I do not believe so. I am of the view that the world is very good. And to be cautious, at least my world is very good. What does it mean? It means that even if the entire world is not good, one can always create his own good world. After all one does not live in the whole world. Your own world is very small and it can always be made good even if you are not able to make the entire world good.

I will explain it further. Kanpur is a dirty city. Kanpurites will excuse me but this is what they themselves say. The effort should be to make Kanpur clean and all should strive for it. But if for some reason, we are not able to do so, what is the option? The option is to keep our mohalla clean, and suppose even that is not possible, the next option is to keep our home clean. Also in order to make the city clean, the process has to be begun from our homes. If homes are not clean, there is no question of the city being clean. After all there are beautiful homes in Kanpur also, staying where one will forget all the dirtiness of Kanpur.

The same is the case with the world also. There are people among whom you will forget all the bad things of this world. You will then see only the good world. Then why not look for these people and be in their company? Who can prevent you from making good friends? After all it is your right to choose your friends, hobbies and lifestyle. This is what constitutes your own small world. And so if the entire world is not beautiful, don't bother. Create your own beautiful world.

Having created your own good, beautiful world, you can proceed, to higher entity (equivalent to mohalla in a town). For a businessman it may be his business circle, for a serviceman it may be his office and so on. Without craving for results, one can always make an effort to make things better at all the places where he goes. This reminds me of a saying by Oscar Wilde which goes like this:

"There are people who create happiness wherever they go, others whenever they go",

Let us belong to the first category of people.

> When someone strikes you, glorify the pain; be grateful that you have a chance to prove your stead fastness and loyalty. A person's test of strength and wisdom rests on this-how great is his sense of equilibrium under stress. A man must have so much balance, so much wisdom that he can withstand all the onslaughts of life.
>
> **Swami Parmananda**

10
WE GET WHAT WE WISH

We get what we wish. But the wish has to be strong. If we wish worldly things, we get worldly things. Wishing is such a strong power that it can overcome all the obstacles. I had a very interesting experience of this fact during my stay in U.K. in 1990. It goes like this.

I went to U.K. in April 1990 to attend a three-month course. The course was held in a small beautiful town of Ilkley near Leeds. All the participants were from India. The town provided an excellent environment for walks and we used to walk around as much as was possible within the time available to us. The town was very neat and clean.

One day I got a penny on the road. The desire reappeared and there was another penny on the road. This way I found many pennies during our walks. Suddenly the wish of finding a pound came to mind. In U.K., no one bothers for a penny but a pound is different. In terms of puchasing power, it is almost equivalent to a twenty-rupee note in India.

I told my friends that since the desire is strong, I should find a pound on the road before the expiry of the course. And the search began. While walking, I looked attentively on the road but to no avail. The highest coin I could find was a five-penny coin. The course was coming to an end. Only a few days were left. Our shopping was also concluding. We had started planning our expenditure carefully. And during one of these last days, while I was returning to my campus, I found a pound on the road. The keen desire was fulfilled. Everyone was thrilled and wanted a party. It was arranged but by pooling more money, and the pound was donated to the local church.

The moral of the incident is that we get what we wish. That being so, why should we wish for lower things? One should wish for higher things and he will get higher things. And ultimately we become what we wish to become.

11
SMALL IS BEAUTIFUL

Many years ago I came across an article published in *The Hindustan Times*. It was titled 'The Gandhian Behind Small is Beautiful'. It sounded very interesting and I went through it.

The article talked about a book *Small is Beautiful,* written by a world-famous economist E F Schumacher. Schumacher was not a laboratory economist. He had been at the helm of affairs of such giant companies as 'British Coal' and had seen the whole world before arriving at certain conclusions which form the basis of his book.

One may be tempted to jump at the conclusion that the book might be raising the commonly talked about issue of big vs small. Yes, it does; but this is not the central theme of the book. Here an economist, for the first time, stressed that human beings had to be treated as human beings, rather than as numbers. He felt that the ordinary people had become fed up with the price that was being extracted from them in the name of 'progress' and 'development'. As a result he gave a set of new ideas that held the promise of relief. These ideas appeared in the form of a book titled *Small is Beautiful.*

I had the occasion to go through this book a few years ago. While going through it, I recollected an interview of Mahatma Gandhi on his economic views. When someone asked about the books on economics read by him, he replied that he had read only one book and that was the Bible. In the Bible also he quoted a sentence which says:

"It is easier for a camel to go through the eye of a needle than for a rich man to enter into the Kingdom of God".

This is all that Gandhiji had read about economics. At that time I could not give much meaning to it. But after having gone through this book, I could clearly see the significance of what Gandhiji had said. Still the doubt persisted about the relevance of small being beautiful in the changed environment. It took me a few more years to believe that the concept of small being beautiful is still relevant and that if human beings are to be treated as human beings, there is no option but to believe only in this concept. However, I am prepared to make one concession in the changed environment and that is to treat 'Small as more Beautiful' as compared to big. In the present write-up, an attempt will be made to put up a case in favour of this belief.

No one will disagree that the purpose of economic development is to create a happier society. Even in our scriptures physical needs have been given preference over other needs. The line 'भूखे भजन न होय गोपाला' conveys this message clearly. We also believe in the theory of 'वासुधैव कुटुंबकम्' (the world is one family). It means that the gains of economic development are to be shared by all members of society. Otherwise, the objective of economic development will not be achieved.

In his book Schumacher gave a detailed data to prove that the present trend of economic development has failed to achieve its objective. In terms of happiness, the world is worse off though physical comforts have increased manifold. What has happened in the name of economic development is the cornering of the earth's scarce resources by the few rich and educated. This is seen at all levels,

The other line of argument advanced by the author is also convincing. He says the earth just does not have enough resources to sustain the kind of economic development, we dream of. After all, where do we fix the standards? Is the consumption of an average American to be taken as the criterion or that of an average Indian? Moreover, even an average American is not satisfied with his consumption level. He is also looking for more, notwithstanding his actual needs. Similarly, within a country, developed or developing, levels of consumption vary so widely that it is difficult to fix a fair criterion. Of late there has been a trend of comparing consumption levels of non-essential items like plastics, paper, energy, etc. What purpose is served by such comparison? Do we mean to condemn those who consume unnecessarily high or laugh at those who can never reach at that level ? In the process we make both of them unhappy. The author has tried to prove by giving actual statistics that it is futile to conceive of a society with such high levels of consumption. It is neither desirable nor possible.

I look at it from another point of view.

We all know that this world has existed for at least several thousand years and may be for million years. In all probability it will exist for as many more years. But can we think of even hundred years ahead, what to say of thousands and millions of years? Almost all of our resources, it is said, will deplete in a couple of decades. What kind of existence therefore do we conceive after the depletion of these so-called essential resources?

With this background we come to the subject of big vs small. Everyone puts forth arguments in favour or against. I feel it should be looked into from the point of view of the objectives to be achieved from economic development. If big delivers these objectives, I am prepared to accept this concept without any argument and if small delivers these objectives, those who believe in big should give up their case.

Let us look at the arguments against the concept of big. The amount of competition it has created is mind-boggling. It can be scientifically proved that it has led to an increase in tensions and separatism in society. Today wars are fought mainly for economic considerations. In the process scarce resources for which we show so much concern are also wasted and we all watch helplessly.

There are many other evils allied to the big concept. Exploitation is the one which comes to my mind immediately. It may be either of the environment, labour, consumers or

Small Is Beautiful

something else. Then there is evasion of taxes, etc., which, in turn, leads to bribery, etc. The human greed thus keeps multiplying and I feel that the big concept has greatly contributed to the fall in human values.

There is a point when the supporters of big theory plead that there is something like economy of scale. There can be no denial of this fact. But then many other costs are added when a shirt or shoe produced in one corner of the world is sold in another corner of the world. In most of the cases, the economy of scale is lost as far as ultimate consumer is concerned. He gets goods at four to five times the cost of production. Then of what use is the economy of scale? It only makes a few individuals excessively rich who further waste scarce resources in the name of progress. And the common man pays the price of their luxuries.

Thus it is amply established that the concept of big does not lead to the fulfilment of the goal of human existence. Therefore, Schumacher advocated the concept of the 'small' which is conducive to peaceful human existence in the long run. Once he said at a conference of big industrialists of Europe: "It is quite certain that if there should be a real resource crisis or a real ecological crisis in this world, the poor people would survive. Whether the rich will survive is much more doubtful. India will survive though whether Bombay will survive is more doubtful. That New York will survive is an impossibility." He then advised his listeners to change their entire outlook and work hard to reverse the trend that modern civilisation has brought about. Attempting to transmit the benefits and 'knowhow' of such a civilisation to the poor countries was foolish for 'overseas' development was really a process where you collect money from the poor people in the rich countries, to give to the rich people in the poor countries. Nobody intended this, but there was blindness about this pattern of living. He, therefore, told his august audience that instead of doling out charity to others, they should concentrate on something more important, i.e., changing themselves. The real solution to the world's problems will be found, he said, when the rich and the educated abandon their present policy of cornering the earth's scarce resources and instead pick up that most important of knowhow, that of survival, from the legacy that the likes of Buddha and Gandhi have left behind. And this legacy is what he called the concept of the 'small'. Be it in the field of industry, business, needs, small is always beautiful or, say, more beautiful.

His colleagues called Schumacher a crank, for his change in thinking but he always reacted with characteristic humour.

"Yes, I know I am called a crank, but I never mind, because a crank is a tool which is simple, small, inexpensive, economical, efficient and it makes revolution."

And there can be no doubt that it is the small incidents and small ideas which have brought about revolutions in all fields. Then what is wrong if we say 'Small is Beautiful'?

Little Words !

"Yes, you did it !" .... "I did not !" ....
Thus the little quarrel started,
Thus by unkind little words
Two fond friends were parted.
"I am sorry !" ... "So am I !"....
Thus the little quarrel ended,
Thus by loving little words
Two fond hearts mended.

12

WE ALL ARE COOLIES

I was posted as Collector of Basti in 1982. It was my first (and the only one) posting as Collector. At that time, Basti used to be the biggest district of U.P. with 32 development blocks. It was predominantly a rural district and the rural population was also the highest in the State. The district had great potential for development. Overall the posting provided an excellent opportunity to serve its people. I tried to take full advantage of this opportunity and derived great satisfaction from it. The people of Basti gave me a lot of affection and goodwill. I still feel very close to them and consider it as one of the most valuable earnings of my life.

However, there was another aspect of the posting. I had a big house with about 10 acres of cultivable land. There was a lot of manpower to look after everything. I had tremendous resources at my command. Lots of people would come to see me every day and most of them gave the impression as if I was the best collector, the district had had till then with one or two exceptions. Almost every office in the district seeks instructions/guidance from the collector at one time or another. Overall it made one feel at the top of the world as if everything really belonged to him.

Fortunately, I had the grace of God and the power never went to my head (at least to my knowledge). Though one did not find much time for leisure in a posting like this, still I used to spend sometime in the back lawns sitting alone or with the family. During one such day, I was thinking about all the opportunities, perks and facilities the post provided to me and that one day all these things would go. It shocked me for a moment because inadvertently, perhaps, I had also developed a feeling of belonging to all these things. Then my thought went to a coolie who quite often carries boxes/packets containing expensive things fully knowing that nothing belonged to him. He was concerned only with the wages after taking the load to its destination. "Am I not like a coolie?" said my inner voice; "Carrying expensive load on my head, may be a box containing gold, which does not belong to me". Why should then there be any sense of belonging? The only thing expected was more care and sincerity when the coolie knew that the load was expensive. But if during the course of carrying the load, he developed a feeling of belonging and refused to part away with the load, the consequence was obvious. This thought process cleansed my mind of all the ego, which developed inadvertently and I could serve the district with much more dedication and detachment during the remaining tenure.

This analogy can be extended to all of us. It appears more obvious in transferable jobs where one starts understanding the temporariness of things rather early. But in other cases also, it is a matter of time only, the time during which the coolie carries the load. One may carry a load up to platform number one and another up to platform number nine. The separation of load and the coolie is a foregone conclusion. All the world, we see around us with a sense of belonging is like the load on the head of a coolie. Those who have good world around them develop a sense of belonging to it (like expensive load) and feel great pain when the time of separation comes. Is it not wise to understand the reality right in the beginning? And the best way is to realise as early as possible that "WE ALL ARE COOLIES" and the load does not belong to us.
- Detachment from the world of objects is not possible without attaching ourselves with something nobler and divine.

13
PLAN YOUR LANDING

Pandit Ram Kinkarji was a well-known saint. He was such a good commentator on the Ramayana that even a staunch atheist was compelled to listen to him attentively. The reason is that he related the story of Ramayana to the common man's day-to-day life in a very convincing manner. This way he did a great service to mankind.

I came in contact with Panditji at a friend's place in Dehradun many years back. Since then I had his blessings and the privilege of his company almost every year till his death. Panditji used to visit Kanpur also for discourses every year. During one such visit I had the opportunity to have a discussion with him. The reference was the suffering of most of the old people despite all their goodness and success in life. Panditji dealt with the subject very convincingly.

The sum and substance of his analysis was that those who do not plan the end of their life's journey usually suffer, irrespective of their success and goodness. In the present write-up, I am trying to put up the same thing in a more elaborate manner.

I compare the journey of life with the flight of an aeroplane. It can be divided into four parts. 1. Moving on the runway; 2. Taking off and gaining height; 3. Flying; 4. Landing.

Life can also be similarly divided into four parts. Taking a good lifespan of eighty years, each part can be assumed approximately equal. During the first twenty years one prepares for the flight of life. He has to run on the ground with adequate acceleration so that he is able to take off before the end of the runway. He cannot venture taking off before acquiring sufficient speed which may lead to crash. This period is called childhood which is preparatory for the flight of life.

Having gained sufficient momentum in the first part of life, one takes off and gains height. This is what we call success in life. A normal person goes up and up during this period of life till he reaches the saturation point. This point varies from person to person depending upon his ambition and circumstances. Likewise, the altitude of an aeroplane depends upon the type of plane, the distance of the destination and the weather. In this phase of life, one has to carefully determine the limits, otherwise the so-called success may turn out to be painful.

The next stage is of flying at a constant altitude with minor variations. This stage is comparable with adulthood when one has achieved all worldly successes and is satisfied with his gains. Those who do not reach the satisfaction level may ultimately lose the pleasure of their gains. Such people become miserable right at this stage of life. They forget that the fuel in the plane is limited to cover more distance at a constant height. This is the best part of the journey. In an aeroplane's journey also, one is most carefree during this period. The food, snacks, etc., are served during this period and there are no restrictions on movement.

The last stage is landing. No pilot can afford to forget that his ultimate destination is ground only. If he forgets that, the consequences need not be told. The same thing has to be remembered in life also but most of us forget this simple fact. Having reached high in the sky, we do not want to come down voluntarily. The obvious consequence is a crash and that is what we call suffering in the last phase of life. This is what Panditji had hinted at.

The preparation for landing has to be started right in the third phase. The belts have to be fastened, movements stopped and descent begun. It is this process of descent which is resisted by most of us. Those who do not, land safely and smoothly meet the end of their life happily without any complaint.

14
THINK POSITIVE

The process of thinking is what differentiates man from animals. It is a wonderful faculty provided by God to human beings. The only thing that makes us a higher animal is the ability to think. And it is the quality of thinking which distinguishes one person from another. Our best friends and our worst enemies are our thoughts. Thoughts make the whole dignity of man. Every action begins with a thought. It may be the starting of a business, construction of a building or killing someone. As are the thoughts, so are the actions. In this write-up we shall briefly discuss the quality aspect of thoughts and their impact on life.

An elderly friend of mine gave me a book many years back. It was titled *The Power of Positive Thinking* written by Norman Vincent Peale. I went through it and found it inspiring. Then after a year or so another friend gave me a book by the same author titled *The Amazing Results of Positive Thinking*. This book contained a large number of real life cases in which positive thinking had done wonders in the lives of people. Subsequently, I came across the whole series of books on positive thinking by the same author and went through them. The present article is mainly the result of this reading coupled with my own personal experiences in life.

In one of these books, I read a case which goes like this: A lady ran a restaurant in San Francisco. It was a beautiful place, full of colour and life. Then her eyesight began to fail. Soon she was blind, living in darkness. One day the telephone rang and she groped her way to answer it and received the shocking news that her husband had just been killed in an accident.

Blindness and now her husband suddenly dead. She sat by the telephone, utterly crushed, wondering what she was going to do. She was dejected for weeks, living in helplessness. But in this most complete darkness, emotionally and physically, she perceived finally, by the help of her strong faith, that there was something positive to which she could attach herself. She did not choose to dwell on the negative, she sought the positive and she found it in a most remarkable way. Putting sincere faith and strong positive thinking against her sad conditions, she determined that she would conquer her grief, loneliness and handicap.

And in due course she not only succeeded but succeeded greatly. She wrote three successful cookbooks and a book of inspiration. She operated a frozen food business with her two sons and went to the office every day.

That is what positive thinking is. It is tough mindedness. It is the refusal to be defeated. It is making the most of what you have to deal within life. It is to look at the positive side of your life and dwell on it. It is to look at the filled part of a half empty glass. We all have positive points in life even in the most gloomy conditions and if the mind can be turned to these, the positive thinking will start by itself. So if you feel that you are defeated and have lost confidence in your ability to win, sit down, take a piece of paper and make a list, not of the factors that are against you, but of those that are for you. If you think constantly of the forces that seem to be against you, you will build them up into a power far beyond that which is justified. They will resume a formidable strength which they do not possess. But if, on the contrary, you mentally visualise and affirm and reaffirm your assests and keep your thoughts on them emphasising them to the fullest extent, you will rise out of any difficulty regardless of what it may be. Your inner powers will reassert themselves and with the help of God, lift you from defeat to victory.

Feeling of confidence depends upon the type of thoughts that habitually occupy your mind. Consider defeat and you are bound to feel defeated. But practise thinking of confident thoughts, make it a dominating habit, and you will develop such a strong sense of capacity that regardless of what difficulties arise you will be able to overcome them. A feeling of confidence actually induces increased strength.

Well, most of us raise the point that all this is easily said than done. True, the blows of life, the accumulation of difficulties, the multiplication of problems tend to sap your energy and leave you spent and discouraged. In such a condition, the true status of your power is often obscured, and you yield to a feeling of discouragement that is not justified by the facts. It is vitally essential to reappraise your personality assets. When done in an attitude of reasonableness, this evaluation will convince you that you are less defeated than you think you are.

The secret is to fill your mind with thoughts of faith, confidence and security. This will force out or expel all thoughts of doubt, all lack of confidence. The situation has to be faced as it exists now. There is no point in regretting the past. Never do it. However the mistakes of the past, if any, are to be converted into opportunities for the future. And this is what you call 'Positive Thinking'. There is always a way to handle your difficulty or problem. A summarised ten steps approach is given below:

i) Thank God you have difficulties. It is a sign of life.
ii) Learn to stand back from your troubles and calmly survey them.
iii) Use your full mind power to analyse your difficulties. Then systematically chip away at it, bit by bit.
iv) Think positively about your difficulty. Believe that you can overcome it. This way you will be on the way to victory.
v) Learn the spiritual-practical method for handling a difficulty.
vi) Work persistently and eventually you will be victorious.
vii) Grow to such heights that you can look down upon your problems.
viii) Calmly take life as it comes. Deal with your difficulties with a controlled mind.

ix) Never build a case against yourself, i.e., never think of failure.
x) Make use of the power of the Almighty. Troubles will defeat you without God, but with His help you can handle any difficulty.

Another problem which one faces in positive thinking is how to sustain positive thoughts. Positive thoughts can be induced in everyone momentarily but that does not help, if they are not sustained. Positive thinking requires training and study and long perseverance. You have to be willing to work at it, sometimes for long. It is like food. It must be taken daily and in healthy doses to keep the body going. You must remember that there is much more power in your personality that has ever been used up. Release it through the process of regular positive thinking. Life is uncertain and it will always remain so (it has an 'if' at the centre of the word). Take it in its stride and live a full life.

Does positive thinking always work? Of course it does; positive thinking will work if you are willing to work at it. It is not an easy discipline. It takes hard work and strong belief. It takes honest living, and a keen desire to succeed. And you will need to keep working at it constantly to achieve success. Just when you believe you have mastered it, you will have to develop it again.

Success is available to all of us if we follow the basic principles of positive thinking. Start now to precondition your mind to success.

> Thought makes the whole dignity of man;
> endeavour to think well, that is the only morality.

15
KEEP THE STRINGS LOOSE

Life is a bondage. This is what is said in the scriptures of all religions. We ourselves feel so in our day-to-day life. Every relationship is a bondage and becomes a cause of our sorrow at one point or the other. We expect happiness out of a relationship and the outcome turns out to be just the opposite. At that time we feel shocked and make our life more unhappy. We start blaming others and tend to become pessimistic. Our trust on others suffers a setback and we become unsure of ourselves.

What to do then? Should we sever all the relationships? In that case the remedy will be worse than the malady. This will amount to escapism. Anyway, all relationships get severed at one point or the other. Then why should we take the responsibility of severing them ourselves. It will make us feel guilty and the very purpose of doing so will be lost. What is the alternative? This is what we shall be discussing in the present write-up.

Everyone is born without bondage but as one grows, one creates bondages in various forms. To begin with, family relations like mother, father, brother, sister, etc., become the bondages. These relations develop a sense of obligation towards each other. Then relations in the form of friends come in life. As one gets married, new relationships come in one's life and then come son and daughter relationships. As one grows in status, the social-relations also become important. One develops a sense of obligation towards society and the corresponding expectation of recognition, name and fame.

On careful examination we will find that all these relationships are bondages as long as they create a feeling of obligation towards one another. If the obligation is not fulfilled from any side, the result is unhappiness. And if these are fulfilled, we suffer the shocks of separation, temporary or permanent. We sometimes miss a very dear person so much that his or her dearness becomes a source of pain for us. This can be compared with the scene when two persons are linked to each other with a tight rope and the rope is suddenly cut. Both of them will experience a great jerk and may even fall on the ground, if taken unaware.

What is the solution of this problem? Should no bonds be developed from the beginning itself? Yes, it is the ideal solution but it is not possible for ordinary mortals. As long as a common man lives in this world, he develops various bondages. In a way these bondages act as a moving force for him and all the physical progress seen by us is the result of such bondages. One develops a bondage for money, another for fame and yet another for social service. They all render useful services to the society and to that extent their bondages are to be appreciated. Here we are talking of a situation when bondage becomes a cause of misery.

At this stage we have to apply discretion. We should be able to judge as to when a particular bondage has ceased to remain useful or a motivating force. We must also remember the fact that all the bondages will sever one day or the other. So why not to prepare ourselves for the same? The best way of doing so is to loosen the strings of our bondages. In that case we shall not get a jerk when they get severed. With loose strings we have the freedom of movement and also the necessary restrain so as not to go astray. Such restrains are necessary for the common man. However, a realised soul need not have any strings at all.

This approach should be adopted in all kinds of bondage. This is the only way of insuring ourselves against the shocks received due to the sudden breaking of various relationships. There may still occur unexpected incidents where we may fail to exercise our discretion. These are to be treated as 'accidents' and we should accept them as such.

- Be prepared for misery in return for your love.
- If you get attached, you become miserable.
- Life is good or evil according to the state of our mind, it is neither by itself.
- What is good for me may be bad for you.
- God gives us relatives. Thank God, we can choose our friends.
- One trouble that jet planes have got us into is that there are no longer any distant relatives.

16
RIDING THE WORLD

Horse riding was compulsory for IAS trainee officers when I joined the Academy in 1975. However not all officers enjoyed this compulsion. Getting up early in the morning, wearing breeches and climbing down the valley to face the generally rude groom hardly pleased anyone of us. Having done all this one had to face an unpredictable animal who was always favoured in case of any lapse on our part. No wonder most of the officers felt that it was not relevant. And their voice has been heard partially as riding is now no longer compulsory for IAS officers.

I have done a lot of thinking about the relevance of horse riding in the training of IAS officers. I have found it very relevant from every point of view. First the sheer physical exercise involved in horse riding keeps one physically fit. Then the horse is a very good means of transport when all other means fail. I have successfully tried it in the administration of Garh Mukteshwar Mela. Even today there are places where one cannot reach even by jeep. Over that the subordinate staff tries to dissuade the officer from undertaking any risk in visiting farflung places. With a horse as a means of travel, they find no reason to do so.

As one assumes district charge, the relevance of riding becomes clearer. It is told during the probation period that a district is like a horse — unpredictable. If anything goes wrong, it is the collector who is held responsible and not the district. Like the four stages of riding: walking, trotting, cantering and galloping, the collector has to come to the command of the district in stages. He has to know when to kick and where, when to pull the reins and how much. Any mismatch may disturb the balance and the rider will either be shaken or may even fall. No purpose is served, then by complaining about others, as only he is held responsible for his fall.

Having crossed all these initial stages of administration, as I look at life in this world, I feel that even this world is like a horse. To enjoy living in this world one should know how to ride it. In this write-up an attempt is being made to compare 'Riding the Horse' with 'Living in the World'.

The first step in riding is mounting. One has to avoid rough, jerky movements as one mounts the pony. These may startle the pony and cause it to shift position, making mounting much harder. In the same fashion the entry to the worldly life has to be smooth. It can also be compared with the take-off of an aeroplane. It has to be smooth and needs proper planning. It is like student life which prepares you for mounting the world. If one does not plan well, he may falter right at the mounting stage itself and then there is no question of riding the world, what to say of enjoying it.

Having mounted the horse, one should learn the techniques of riding. The first stage is proper positioning. It includes holding the reins and sitting properly. This is quite important for the next stage, that is pacing. In this world also one has to be in command as well as in a state of alertness. The world has to be faced with confidence. 'Be careful but not fearful' should be the guiding factor. Having mounted and taken a comfortable and alert position, one is ready for pacing.

You cannot run very fast right from the beginning. It has to be in stages. The first stage is 'The Walk'. In this stage the rider should hold his head high and focus his eyes straight ahead but the hands and body should move slightly in response to the horse's movement. This is the stage when you judge the world and the world judges you. If the going is smooth one can shift to the next stage which is 'The Trot'. This is the most important stage and a very active pace. The rider must learn to rise from the saddle as one diagonal hits the ground and sit back as the other comes down. Once you have learnt the rising trot you will never forget it but it takes a lot of practice.

In worldly life also it is the most important stage. One must learn to rise and sit with the world and if one does not or does so out of phase, the result will be painful. You will be hit here and there and may have to be out of the race. No purpose will be served by blaming the world for everyone will only blame you. The world will always behave like that. It is you who has to learn rising and sitting in the ups and downs of the world and in the same phase.

Having properly learnt the stage of 'The Trot', one enters the stage, called 'The Canter'. In this stage the rider should sit well down in the saddle and his hands and body should follow the rhythm of the pony as it canters along. He has no longer to rise up and sit back with pony. The world too behaves in a similar way once you cross the trotting stage. Having braved the ups and downs of the world, you learn to be in rhythm with it and then the ups and downs of the world no longer bother you. You have just to sit well down in the saddle and let the world run itself while you enjoy the riding best.

The last stage is 'The Gallop'. The gallop is simply a fast canter. When galloping, the rider should not allow his weight to fall on the pony's back. He has to lean forward and raise himself just clear of the saddle. His back should be straight, head up and shoulders forward. He should support his weight on his knees and feet. Is it not the same with the world also? Having fallen in the rhythm with the world, a stage comes when one rises above it. He has no more to sit over it. That is to say, that he is unaffected by the world though still being in it. This is the ultimate in the riding of the world as well as the horse.

Having mastered these stages, riding becomes merely a pleasure, a sport or whatever name you may give it. One can even carry out various exercises while being on the horse and horse will behave the way you want it to. So is the case with the world; once you master it, it becomes your slave and if you allow it to master you, you remain a slave of the world.

Riding The World

Having enjoyed riding, one has to dismount. The pony is to be brought to a halt. The feet are to be taken out of the stirrups. Leaning forward with both hands, you have to drop lightly to the ground. The reins still being in your hand, you handover the horse back to the groom. In the same fashion, one should retire from the world in a dignified manner, handing it over to the next generation.

Is riding not relevant for all of us to enjoy living in this world ?

- A man of wisdom lives in the world but the world does not live in him.
- It's always been and always will be the same in the world : The horse does the work and the coachman is tipped.
- The life of the world is but a sport and a pastime.
- The only true method of action in this world is to be in it, but not of it.
- The world is a form of our thoughts.
- The world will not change. You have to change yourself.
- Understand what this world is so that it may not hurt you.

17
REFUSE TO BE POOR

What is the difference between a rich and a poor person? It is a question difficult to answer in definite terms. The answer will vary from person to person, from situation to situation and also upon the way one looks at the question. Rich and poor are not absolute terms. They are relative. However, we shall define here richness as that level of prosperity, at which one is able to comfortably meet his personal and social needs. Unfortunately, most of those persons also who fall under this definition of richness, consider themselves to be poor. This article is mainly addressed to them.

Let us have a look at the requirements of a rich man. His basic three needs of food, clothing and shelter are the same as that of any other person. Maybe the quality of food consumed, clothes worn and houses lived in would be better than that of a so-called poor person. But in quantity he is most likely to consume less as far as food is concerned. He will either have no time to eat properly or will have dietary restrictions, self-imposed or imposed by the doctor. I have a very close doctor friend whose wife is also a practising doctor. They earn lakhs of rupees every month. But they have hardly time to eat their food properly. So much so that sometimes even we have to starve when we are their guests. Another factor related to food is its cooking. A rich man in all likelihood eats food cooked not by his wife or mother but by a servant. The thoughts which go along with the cooking of food are very important. These days servants very rarely have true loyalty to their masters. Cooking is just a paid job for them and they have no love for it. Their interest is better served if the family members do not eat properly. They are hardly bothered if the food cooked by them is relished or not.

Another aspect of eating food is whether the family members eat together at the dining table. It is generally seen that a rich family is more individualistic and each of its member has his own time for eating food. Thus the entire family is hardly able to meet at the dining table. This way they miss a great opportunity to come closer to each other and also to enjoy the food.

Then there is the question of appetite. Rich people are generally caught up in so many worries that they have no appetite for food. Eating is just a part of their engagement sheet and not an essential part of living. They forget that the very purpose of earning more and more is defeated if they are not able to take genuine care of their health.

Coming to clothing, no doubt a rich man will have a large number of clothes and expensive ones. But the basic question is, can anyone wear more than what is required at a point of time? One cannot wear two shirts at a time, nor two pairs of shoes. However, I can say with certainty that a poor man enjoys his good clothes more than the rich man. Getting a new suit stitched brings much more pleasure to a poor man than by a rich person procuring ten new suits. Even a new shirt will give him immense pleasure which a rich person cannot think of. The same is the case with shoes, sarees, jewellery, etc.

When we look at the problems in maintaining a large number of items, I feel it is not worth it. For example, if one has, say, four pairs of shoes, every morning he has to decide which one to wear. There is always a conflict in mind when one has to choose. Then the one intended to be worn may need polishing. For a variety of shoes one will have to keep a variety of polishes and brushes. A poor man has no such worries and feels quite happy with his limited possession.

Factors like cost of maintenance, fear of getting spoiled, fear of theft and even the worry of disposal are additional botherations of a rich person who has a large number of expensive items. In all probability, his possessions remain showpieces because they are never used to an extent which makes them disposable. On the other hand, a poor person's possessions find utility even after he has used them. He has no hesitation in passing them to a poorer person after using it himself.

More or less the same arguments apply to shelter also. One cannot sleep on two beds at the same time, leave alone two rooms. Today no one wants to have a large number of children, specially the rich. Also a rich man generally does not entertain his guests at home. Then of what use is the big house? Its furnishing, maintenance, taxes and envy of the neighbours will always be a cause of worry. The size of the house is also likely to keep his real well-wishers away and chances are that he will remain surrounded by sycophants only. The most important fact is that a rich man will hardly have any time to enjoy his large house. He may have a big lawn but may not have time to sit there. He may have a swimming pool but no time to swim.

On the other hand, a modest house will always be enjoyed more. It can be maintained properly without much external help. It can be furnished easily. The guests are generally welcome in such houses and one can really enjoy the company of well-wishers. A rich man may not be able to sleep in his big house without sleeping pills whereas a poor person will have sound sleep in his modest house.

Thus we find that in the three essential aspects of life, a poor person is somewhat better placed as compared to a rich person. In other aspects of life, he may be lacking. There may be few rich persons who may be really better off than a poor person in the essential aspects of life but that is mainly due to their way of thinking rather than their wealth.

Now a few words about those aspects of life where a so-called poor person may feel lacking. These may be the areas like liberal use of car, eating in good restaurants, presenting gifts, or holidaying. Here a wise person should analyse whether such desires are merely for impressing others or are genuine needs. If it is the former then such a person is bound to invite trouble for himself and nothing can be done about it. However, if they are genuine needs, my experience is that one can afford to be liberal in these areas also by proper planning. For example, while using a car one can plan a journey in such a manner that many destinations are covered in one trip. Similarly, eating outside can be an occasion on which one would spend otherwise also. In the matter of gifts, purchasing at suitable occasions or making proper use of the gifts received is of great help. Holidaying can be made very much economical if timely planning is done and one does not feel tempted to do unnecessary shopping while holidaying. The point being made is that even in these aspects of life, one need not feel poor.

The idea here is not to condemn richness but to condemn the feeling of being poor. Riches do make a difference in life. Money is important and it changes the quality of life. In today's context, it is more so. But overall it makes only a marginal difference, say, ten per cent. It is again emphasised that here poor means those who consider themselves poor despite being able to meet all their essential personal and social needs.

So, friends, stop feeling poor. The difference between you and the rich is only marginal, about ten per cent. An additional ten per cent will make you rich provided you are mentally rich. Enjoy what you have rather than fret and fume about what you do not have. It is the total quality of life which should be taken into account and not a lopsided view of it. And if, you do so, you will have no cause to complain. You will also feel rich and will 'Refuse to be Poor'.

18
ARE YOU OKAY ?

Every day, all of us come across friends, relatives and acquaintances who ask whether we are okay and we mostly reply in the affirmative. Perhaps no one wants to hear the contrary. One day, while on a tour of Kanpur, I was on my morning walk, when a good friend of mine asked the same question. I was really not okay that day and for a change I wanted to speak the truth. So I asked my friend whether he wanted me to speak the truth. Somewhat bewildered he looked at me and I explained to him further. In case he wanted me to speak a lie, the reply was in the affirmative. But if he wanted me to speak the truth, the reply was in the negative and I needed sometime to explain my problem. He was obviously not prepared for that and the matter ended there.

However, this set me thinking: 'Are we really okay?' when we say so and I arrived at the conclusion that it was not so. Most of us are not okay when we say so. The point to be pondered upon is why it is so. The obvious reason is that in this modern world everyone is so busy with himself that he has no time to listen to others' problems, and lives alone for the problems of his own family members, including wife and children. Most of us are so busy in earning our living, that in the process we forget to live itself.

I fail to understand that if one is not able to talk about his problems with his relatives and friends, is it really worth calling them relations and friends? After all, what is the purpose of having relatives and friends? I feel the purpose is to share our joys and sorrows with them. That is why there is the custom of inviting and informing friends and relatives on both type of occasions. It is said that joy is multiplied and sorrow is divided by sharing. Does it really happen in today's society? I don't think so. On the other hand, the joy may reduce or may turn out to be disharmonious in the company of opportunistic friends and relatives, while the sorrow may multiply by all sorts of advice offered by them. Obviously, sharing loses its meaning in both cases.

All this leads to tension at individual level and consequently at the social level. The child is not able to convey his problems to his or her parents. Even the husband finds no time to listen to his wife's problems and then the chain reaction starts. Husbands, wives and children are parts of society and they carry tensions wherever they go. The result is that we find a disharmonious environment everywhere. Be it a school, a bank, an office or a bus, there is always a lack of courtesy and accepting a little inconvenience for the sake of others is nowhere seen.

What do we do then? Curse others and suffer? This remedy is worse than the malady. No, this is not the solution to the problem. The solution has to be sought within oneself. Am I really concerned about the joys and sorrows of others? Seek an honest answer from within. If the answer is no, there is no need to feel guilty about it. No beginning is too late. Start from your family. Are you really aware of the problems of your wife and children? If not, talk to them lovingly. Most of the problems have no solutions. They are just to be shared. Every problem is an opportunity to improve. Similarly, share their joys too. An occasional word of sincere appreciation can do wonders. It is more than an ornament. Many a time the grievance may not be reasonable. But listen to it patiently and even accommodate against your logic for the sake of harmony. It is worth the sacrifice.

Once harmony at home is established, every member of the family will act as a nucleus of positive thinking. Sharing the joys and sorrows of others is possible only when one is harmonious within oneself. Be genuinely interested in others. Be lavish in your appreciation of others, genuinely happy in their joys and truly concerned in their sorrow. You will then find many who will reciprocate in the same way. Then you need not carry the load of your joys and sorrows alone on your head. It will lighten your burden. You will then be able to say that you are not okay, if it is so and there will be no need to tell a lie. There will be well-wishers who will have time for you when you need them. In all probability you will then always be okay.

- Be openly happy in the joy of others. Be sincerely sympathetic in others' sorrow. This is the true joy.
- Great joys, like griefs, are silent.
- He who has transcended egoism, experiences everlasting joy.
- Kindness is an attitude of sympathy along with love and understanding.
- Kindness is returned in kindness, ninety per cent.
- Kindness is the oil that takes the friction out of life.
- Little deeds of kindness, little words of love, help make the earth happy, like the heaven above.

19
SECULARISM AND NATIONAL DEVELOPMENT

In the history of Independent India, the role of religion has come up as a major issue. It appears that the future of the country is linked with it. People have begun to wonder whether the adoption of secularism under the Indian Constitution was a right step. A great portion of national resources is being spent in containing the fire of communalism. A wall has arisen between communities which have been living like brothers for centuries. This has had adverse effects on the economic and social progress of the country. If this situation is not controlled soon, the very existence of the nation may be in danger.

Let us try to understand what is meant by religion. If the role of religion is considered rightly, all problems relating to it will be solved. The scriptures say that religion is something to guide one's conduct in life. As a constitution is required for running an organisation or government, in the same way religion is necessary to live life harmoniously. 'Thus religion may be called the constitution of life and is an internal need of man. The principles laid down in our scriptures are not the dictates of an individual person; they embody the experiences of elevated souls. Some of the principles were relevant in the periods when they were enunciated and now need amendment. It is like amendments in the constitution of a country from time to time as circumstances change. However, the preamble of the constitution remains the same. That is why different practices were advocated in different religions. The amendments were not due to there being anything wrong with the original principles. Human life is subject to change and therefore some principles of life also change. If this is not done, people will abandon religion and the very purpose of religion will be lost.

The basic principles of religion have been reinterpreted from time to time. This led to the birth of different religions. If we look upon various religions from this viewpoint, we will develop reverence for all of them. The principle of secularism was adopted in India keeping this in mind. The framers of the Constitution knew the realities of the country's social structure. They felt that the principle of secularism was needed to meet the changing situation. What we should consider is where things have gone wrong and why the principle of secularism is being questioned. Our Constitution is only about 50 years old. In the history of a country, this is a short period. It is a matter of concern if an important basic principle of our Constitution is being questioned in such a short time.

In order to analyse the situation, we should examine the reasons why people misunderstand or misinterpret religion. We may classify them in four categories: scientific, economic, political and social.

We all are aware of the revolution that has come about all over the world in the field of science. Scientific progress in the past 50 years has been greater than in the previous 2000 years. This has affected human life. The change was so fast that man was not ready for it. Darwin's Theory of Evolution tells us that internal change (physical and intellectual) in human beings takes place gradually in accordance with environment. If external change is very fast, there occurs a gap between it and internal change. This is what has happened in present times. Internal change has not been able to keep pace with the change in the external environment. We may also say that religion has not been able to keep pace with the change in the field of science. This has led to the feeling that religion is a symbol of backwardness and that secularism is opposed to religion. The problem started from here.

For some time people did not realise the consequences of what was happening because the glamour of scientific progress diverted their attention from the fundamental principles of life. They felt that science had answers to all their problems of life. But when they realised the limitations of science, they again turned to the fundamental principles of life which we call religion. Unfortunately, during this period propagation of religion had gone into the hands of people who could not interpret religion in a scientific manner, and people were not prepared to accept the traditional approach. This gave rise to conflict between science and religion. The common man thought it to be a limitation of religion.

The economic revolution all over the world has also affected religion. Religion emphasises the need to reduce one's desires and practise sacrifice. But economic progress implies multiplication of needs. Today the scale of progress of a nation is judged by its consumption level. For this, per capita consumption of items like paper, plastic, energy, etc., is compared. Economic development is also viewed from parameters like gross national Income or Per Capita Income. To raise the poor above the poverty line is considered an important economic programme. For this, various schemes are formulated and targets fixed. All this gives the impression that there is a conflict between economic development and religion, because if the principles of religion are adopted, there would be no need of economic development. In reality, it is not so and there is need to remove this impression. Preachers of religion did not do this, which created a wrong impression about religion.

Changes in the field of politics have also affected religion greatly. Under the Constitution, we have accepted a democratic structure. As long as there was no degradation of political values, religion was not misused in politics. However, as votes are becoming important, religion is being exploited politically. This is being done in several ways. At times it is done by giving undue liberty to a particular community and sometimes by instigating one community against another. Both the situations are unfortunate. This has created a narrow approach to religion.

Similarly, changes in social values have affected religion adversely. In today's society, achievement of success means everything. Be it in the field of education, trade, science or industry, means have become secondary to goals. Whatever means lead to goals quickly are considered acceptable. Even harming others is not considered bad if it is found helpful. In this rat race people think of only self-interest. But religion tells us to think only of the welfare of others. So much so even harming oneself for the sake of others is advocated. Thus there is a conflict between the prevailing norms of society and the principles of religion.

Thus a common man today takes a very narrow view of religion and instead of considering it something essential he believes that it is a hurdle. Therefore, there is need to define and propagate religion properly. In present times, religion will have to be defined scientifically to show that it is an essential need and not a hurdle in the economic, social and political fields. It is not that religion has not been defined in this manner. Many have worked and many more are working in this direction. But unfortunately their message is not being spread sufficiently. Today people raise questions to which religion must provide suitable answers. Otherwise they will have a false view of religion and they cannot be blamed for this. For this, those people are to be blamed who consider themselves to be guardians of religion.

Today science has no conflict with religion. Even in ancient time, scientific progress had reached great heights and using scientific facilities was not considered anti-religion. In fact, proper use of such facilities helps in leading a religious life. Today we are able to do many things much more conveniently which was not possible in earlier times. Religion is, however, against too much dependence on scientific facilities because this could be harmful. That is to say, it is essential to have control over oneself so that one does not become a slave of the products of science. Otherwise science may become a cause of misery. Religion and science are complementary to each other and whenever proper coordination is kept between them, life becomes more pleasurable, at the individual and social levels.

Similarly, there is no conflict between economic development and religion. Every religion advocates that the basic needs of man should be met first, because the mind cannot be healthy unless the body is healthy. Taking proper care of the body is a religious act. However, today economic development is considered to be consuming more resources than needed. This is improper at the individual and social levels. The mind of a man who consumes more than what is required can never be at peace. It affects himself and society adversely. The earth has enough resources to meet the needs, but not the greed of all. Programmes of eradication of poverty point towards the fact that the distribution of resources should be uniform as it is in a family for the whole world is itself a family. Will this lead to economic stagnation? The answer is a clear no. When all members of a society get an opportunity to lead a life which enables them to meet their essential needs, economic development will be very fast. Today the majority of people in the world are poor. This has affected economic development adversely and given rise to tensions due to income disparities. Religion advocates reduction of desires because the earth's resources meet only the essential needs. Today's man may use these resources beyond his needs for a limited period but he will be creating problems for future generations. Excessive use of resources is against nature and creates problems of pollution. Therefore, it becomes clear that there is no conflict between religion and economic development. In fact, economic development will accelerate if we follow the principles of religion.

In the field of politics, use of religion has become a controversial issue. We know that in ancient times, kings used to honour spiritual masters and also acted upon their advice. It shows that religion has always had a role in politics. Gandhiji believed that it is not possible to separate religion from politics. But what kind of religion are we talking about? A religion which has been distorted should have no place in politics. Selfish people who interfere in politics in the name of religion also should have no role to play in this field. Religion can have a place in politics only when these two factors are not there. Gandhiji used to talk about synthesis between religion and politics in this light. We all know that whenever there has been proper coordination between religion and politics society has remained harmonious. But if selfish elements drag religion into politics, it is natural to question the role of religion in politics.

Today several evils have crept into society affecting life adversely. Most people feel that religion is incapable of removing these evils. Whether it is the caste system, untouchability or the dowry tradition, the fact is that there was a rational for them. However, religious leaders did not try to explain the reasons behind these practices nor did they amend them in changing social conditions. On the other hand, these practices took an ugly shape and the people hold religion responsible for it. The truth of the matter is that no religion supports these social evils and there is no place for them in religious conduct. Religion cannot be held responsible for them. The same can be said about the rituals propagated by religion. These also had a scientific basis, though they were not properly explained or amended. For this reason there has been difficulty in understanding religion.

Today there is need to place religion in its right perspective. Discussion on the principle of secularism can be fruitful only when we understand the correct definition of religion. This work cannot be left to the preachers of religion; every responsible section of society will have to come forward for this purpose. Religion is not something which can be understood only by reading books or talking about it at religious places. Religion is something which has to be adopted every moment in daily life. On the surface different religions may look different but their fundamental principles are the same and they tell us the way to lead a meaningful life.

Whenever society has followed religion in its right form there has been prosperity and happiness. The talk of Ram Rajya hints towards this fact. Here Ram should not be taken as a particular person but should be related to his moral principles and these principles are not the property of any particular person or religion. All religions have accepted them fundamentally. The essential nature of man is religious. But due to the ill-effects of the external environment, society has misunderstood it. There is need of correcting the environment and this can be done only when religion is put before society in practical shape. Then only shall we be able to say that religion is not something to be imposed but that a meaningful life cannot be imagined without religion.

Having cleared the ground, we can now discuss the principles of secularism. Keeping in view the diversity of Indian society the framers of our Constitution adopted the principle of secularism. It was not only an immediate need but a long-term goal. Its purpose was to give religious freedom to every citizen of the country; the state was not to interfere in this freedom. Gradually, the definition of secularism has acquired the meaning of "No Religion" instead of "Any Religion". This situation is unfortunate. The main reason for it is the narrowness of preachers of religion and misuse of religion by selfish elements. The majority of our countrymen are illiterate. It is easy to play with their sentiments in the name of religion. This has been fully exploited by selfish elements. This has been particularly done in the field of politics. Most communal riots have resulted from it. Thus the selfish elements have harmed the cause of religion, resulting in a fragmentation of the country. Followers of every religion feel that their religion is being neglected whether they belong to a minority community or the majority community. This has killed the spirit expressed in our Constitution.

Now the time has come when the principle of secularism should be defined in a new perspective. First of all, society has to accept the need for religion which should be defined scientifically. Secularism should mean 'any religion' instead of 'no religion'. Rational thinkers of every religion should be encouraged to define their religion scientifically and to establish harmony with other religions. Today the means of communication are so developed that the message can be spread very easily. The state may even consider using the media at its disposal to propagate the fundamental principles of different religions. This will remove the misunderstandings between different religions. However, this should be done impartially. No doubt it is a difficult thing but it will have a good effect in the long run. No religion should be given so much liberty that it harms the nation or any other religion. On the basis of past experience it can be said that impartial and judicial decisions are never opposed by the people at large. But if a decision does not meet this criteria, it has an adverse effect even on those who are thought to be favoured by it. Any policy of appeasement should be opposed right away. If we don't understand this fact now, it may be too late.

In the present set-up, it is natural for the minority communities to experience a sense of insecurity. Fortunately, in this country the roots of the religion of the majority community are so deep that there should be no fear of any harm coming from it. Its religion is liberal and narrowness has no place in it. If there is any narrowness, it is mainly due to internal weaknesses which should be removed. However, if the majority community is worried about its religion, it indicates that the principle of secularism has not been followed in the right spirit. To that extent its grievances should be taken seriously. If assured of this, its narrowness will go away automatically. It understands the social reality and knows that there is no alternative but to live with people of all religions. If the division of country at the time of independence could not solve this problem, how can any further division do so? Mahatma Gandhi understood this fact very well and opposed division. Therefore there is no alternative to the principle of secularism for our country.

Is secularism only a social compulsion or is it necessary for national development also? The experiences of our own as well as of other nations show that whenever the rulers followed the principle of secularism, development of the countries was fast. If we study ancient history, we learn that the principle of secularism was followed in its true sense. We do not find mention of any religious disputes during the time of Ashoka, Chandragupta, Harsha, etc., which are known for economic and social prosperity. Even in the medieval period we can compare the rules of Akbar and Aurangzeb from this viewpoint. Akbar followed the principle of secularism and propounded Din-e-Ilahi. The reign of Akbar is known for its prosperity. However, the rule of the Mughals came to an end due to the bigotry of Aurangzeb. Most of Aurangzeb's energy was spent in struggling with other religions. In modern times, countries following the policy of bigotry are lagging from the economic and social viewpoints.

Secularism is all the more important for the development of a nation like India. Our social structure is such that people of different religions are related to one another in several ways. Whenever attempts were made to separate them on any issue, the nation had to pay a heavy price and it slid back on the path of development. The problems facing the nation are so complex that raising disputes in the name of religion will be suicidal. We all are aware of the price being paid by us on account of religious disputes. The hidden price of such disputes is much more than what is visible. Our international image also suffers. This affects national development adversely. Economically we have gone back so much that the situation will not improve in the near future. Our narrowness in following the principle of secularism is greatly responsible for this situation. The tragedy is that those who want to take advantage of this narrowness end up becoming its victims.

Does all this mean that our nation has no future? This is not so at all. The roots of Indian society are very strong. Today every responsible section of society is worried over the communal problem. This is an indication of the fact that we want to set things right. To think that people of different religions cannot live together in this country is not true. The problem which looks so gigantic exists only among few people who are exploited by selfish elements. The majority of people of different religions live together in a congenial environment. Therefore, to think that the principle of secularism cannot succeed in this country is wrong. However, it can be followed in right spirit only when the nation is strong and the rulers give up the policy of appeasement. There is a need to deal harshly with people who are engaged in selfish ends in the garb of religion. It should not matter to which religion they belong. Thus, while the principle of secularism is necessary for the development of a nation only a developed and strong nation can become truly secular. The common man understands this very well and this is why the future is hopeful.

> Each soul is potentially divine. The goal is to manifest this divinity within by controlling nature, external and internal. This is the whole of religion.
> *Swami Vivekanand*

20
NO NEED OF ANGER

So much is said and written about anger. *The Oxford Dictionary* defines anger as extreme displeasure. It is always considered to be an undesirable trait. While it is very obvious when taken from religious, spiritual, moral or physical point of view, it is not so when seen from worldly viewpoint. One tends to feel that in a world we face today, it is difficult to survive without anger. Perhaps I also used to feel that way and I used to be angry quite often. It is not that this has been completely won over, but the frequency has reduced greatly. It has not been so as a matter of surrender or helplessness but definitely as a result of wisdom and experience. Now I am of firm belief that anger is not needed even from worldly viewpoint. This is what we are going to discuss in this write-up.

First of all, let us analyse the cause of anger. Whenever we face a situation which is not to our liking, anger is the result. Therefore, in order to avoid the cause of anger, we should always face situations to our liking. Obviously it is not possible. One may have control over oneself but it is not possible on others. Moreover a situation liked by us may not be liked by others and vice versa. That is to say, that we have to often face situations which we may not like and they become the cause of our anger. It may be indiscipline of a subordinate, disobedience by children, a reprimand from the boss, misbehaviour of a shopkeeper, sudden absence of a servant, a traffic jam, long waiting for a bus or train, etc. There can be countless such occasions which may not be to our liking and are potential causes of our anger.

All this means that in our lives, causes of anger are always present. Does it mean that we should be angry whenever such a situation arises? Let us see how that helps. First of all, let us recall that anger means extreme displeasure and not merely displeasure. Here the word 'extreme' is important. I cannot remember even a single incidence in my life where expressing anger helped. The simple reason is that one becomes more vulnerable after expressing anger. This helps neither the person nor the situation. The moment one gets angry, he loses his discriminating power and chances of taking wrong decisions or actions increase. In all probability the angry person ends up suffering more than he would have normally suffered.

One may now ask whether feeling angry and not expressing it would be a better proposition. It is certainly better than the earlier situation but even in feeling angry one suffers. Firstly, it is not good for health and, secondly, it also impairs one's discriminating power. The anger always takes away objectivity.

Then how should one behave in such situations? I think the answer lies in the definition of 'anger' itself. It says anger is 'extreme displeasure'. I feel by removing the word 'extreme' we get the answer. It means there is no harm in feeling displeased in a situation which you do not like. There is no harm in expressing your displeasure in a suitable manner. In fact, it should be done. Whether it is your child, subordinate or any member of the society, whenever situation demands, displeasure should be expressed in a suitable way. Here it will be advisable to remember the famous proverb "Truth should be spoken pleasantly and unpleasant truth should not be spoken." In all likelihood a pleasantly spoken truth will help both you and the situation. The secret is that when you are not extremely displeased you do not lose your discrimination. In that situation, it is possible to take even strict action without any harmful effect.

A more important question is how to avoid anger. This cannot be done suddenly. One has to gain wisdom as well as experience to win over anger. However, reading of good literature, attending discourses of saintly persons and avoiding situations which are likely to cause anger always accelerate the process. Here, I will mention about a talk on the subject "Burn Anger Before Anger Burns You" by Dada J P Vasvani delivered in Delhi in October, 1991. Subsequently it has appeared in the form of a book also. I had the opportunity to listen to him and he summarised his talk beautifully by suggesting ten points for controlling anger. These are given below :

1) Realise that every being is part of God. If so, there is no place for anger as one does not lose temper on oneself.
2) See the grace of God in all happenings. Who knows that a situation causing anger in you may be a blessing in disguise?
3) Develop forgiveness. Understand that most of the time the person appearing to provoke you, has no such intentions. Even if it is so, forgive him. It will defeat his purpose.
4) Keep silent. It very often burns anger.
5) Think from the viewpoint of the other person. Believe that no single viewpoint is absolute. There may be other viewpoints too. You will then not be angry if your viewpoint is not accepted.
6) Do not overload yourself or feel overloaded. This is one great cause of anger. Attend to one matter at a time. The rest can wait. In any case, it is of no use worrying about them while dealing with one.
7) Avoid haste. Plan your work properly so that there is no need of haste. It is hurry, worry and curry that kill a person.
8) Avoid the unpleasant situations. Quite often the anger can be avoided by avoiding the situation. There is no harm in leaving the scene causing irritation.
9) Recite a mantra. This a very powerful way of overcoming anger. Your mind gets occupied with better thoughts.
10) Count numbers. If you are angry count up to ten and if very angry, count up to hundred.

These are some very useful and practical tips and if one is really concerned about his anger, these may be of great help. In the end, I would like to mention another famous proverb about anger which is like this:

"If you are right, you can afford not to be angry.
If you are wrong, you cannot afford to be angry."
Thus there is no need of anger in any situation.

- Anger is a wind which blows out the lamp of the mind.
- Anger is an arrow which will return against you.
  Anger is like short circuit of thoughts. The consequence is darkness.
- Anger is nothing but an attachment for an object.
- Anger is only one letter short of danger.
- Anyone who angers you conquers you.
- For every 10 minutes you are angry ; You lose 600 seconds of happiness !
- He who is slow to anger is better than the mighty.
- Keep cool, anger is not an answer.
- Never write a letter when you are angry.
- Steel loses much of its value when it loses its temper.

21
WHEN YOU LOSE

In the competitive world of today everyone wants to be a winner. In the process we forget that even the thought of winning implies that someone has to lose. Many years ago, I had the occasion of listening to Shri J Krishnamurti. During his talk, he mentioned about competition and compared it to killing. He said that the moment one talks about competition, he kills someone. Here 'killing' should not be taken in its literal sense but the statement definitely gives a message. And the message is that as long as there are winners, there will be losers too and may be more in number than the winners. The tragedy is that we not only ignore the losers, we are callous towards them. Whether it is a losing cricket team or a defeated candidate or someone who has failed to qualify in a competitive examination, this kind of attitude is observed in all the cases. While undoubtedly the winners should get credit, the attitude towards losers also needs change. More important than the attitude of others is the attitude of the loser towards himself. In this write-up we shall discuss a situation when you yourself are a loser.

There is a famous proverb which says, "The glory is in the race run and not in the race won". There is a great message in this. Obviously, here we are talking about those losers who participate in the race but do not win. But it is because of them that the winner wins. In a way they are as much responsible for the victory of the winner as the winner himself. Not only this, they help him excel his performance. Both are essential consituents of the race. No one can be there without the other.

The beauty of the race will be lost without anyone of them. Therefore, the winners and the losers are equally important. The winner will cease to be a winner, if the loser ceases to be a loser. Thus both coexist.

The same logic applies to the race of life. There are winning as well as losing moments in life. We welcome the winning moments and ignore the losing ones. We boast of our good moments and curse the losing ones. But is it fair to do so? Can there be life with good moments only? Good moments will lose their significance without bad moments. They are there only because of bad moments. Without any of them there will be no life, or, say, life will be tasteless. Just as no painting can be made by using only the white colour, so there can be no life consisting of good moments only. We need at least two colours, namely, black and white, in order to make a painting.

Having realised that good and bad moments are essential constituents of life, we should change our attitude towards both. While the good moments of life are to be lived with joy, the bad ones are to be lived with patience and introspection. However our mental attitude towards both should be the same. None of them is going to stay for ever. Good moments are as much fleeting as bad moments. We feel happy during good moments and unhappy whenever they go. Similarly we feel unhappy during bad moments and happy whenever they go. Since both of them have to go eventually the net effect of both is the same. It is just a matter of sequence. In a way bad moments are better than good moments because they end up with happiness while the latter end up with unhappiness. Do we not say that all is well that ends well. If bad moments end well, should they not be more welcome?

If we honestly analyse the good and bad moments of our lives, we will come to the conclusion that bad moments enrich the life more than the good moments. The chances of deviation from the righteous path are greater during good moments than during bad moments. Our real friends are likely to get distanced during good times while bad times bring them closer. A famous proverb in this regard goes like this : "In prosperity your friends know you and in adversity you know your friends". I feel, this is hundred per cent true. Similarly the ego developed during good times does us great harm for a long time and it needs a long spell of bad times in order to go. A wise man should therefore treat both good and bad with equanimity. He should make his life enriching out of both and live out both gracefully.

However, it is not so simple as is made out to be particularly in bad times. While it is easier to maintain equanimity during good times, it is not so easy in bad times. Bad times are the real testing ground and if lacking in inner strength, one tends to break down. There are occasions in life when bad times come for no fault of ours and when we least expect them. They shake us and shake our faith too. How should we face them? Whom should we look to during such times.

I read two books *When Bad Things Happen to Good People* and *Who Needs God* by Harold Kushner sometime back. These books are meant for persons facing such bad moments. In our moments of despair, says the author, it is God, who comes to our rescue, if we are really on the righteous path. And God does not do any magic but helps us in the form of an idea, courage, a well meaning friend, a caring doctor, etc. Then such moments become turning points in the lives of good people. They find a meaning in their tragedies and are able to welcome them too. History is full of stories where greatness was the result of adversity.

Thus we come to the conclusion that the bad moments of life are as important as the good moments, nay, they are more important. Does this not erase the distinction between winners and losers? But this is for those who run the race with zeal, no matter whether they win or lose. You may be one of the losers but never lose your heart. The best thing you can do when you lose is to look victorious. This way you can turn losses into gains and make yourself more envious, than the winner.

22
BE FAIR TO GOD

Almost everyone of us questions the fairness of God at one time or the other in life. So when an advertisement appeared in the newspaper about a talk on the subject 'IS GOD FAIR' by Dada J P Vaswani, it drew my attention too. It was on 16 March, 1993 at the All India Institute of Medical Science Auditorium at New Delhi. Though I reached there in time, the auditorium was full to its capacity and I had to take a seat in the balcony which too became full after sometime. Why I am mentioning this is to indicate that most of us question the fairness of God and want to confirm our views. The talk was inaugurated by Shri L K Advani, who spoke very well and raised some very interesting points. He said we should expect fairness from God only when we are fair to Him. Expecting fairness in return for our unfairness will be to demand injustice from the Supreme Power. And therefore the question to ask should be whether we are fair. This appealed to me very much and I thought of summing up the talk of Dadaji under the title 'Be Fair to God'.

In the life of everyone good as well as bad things come. We happily accept the good things and never question whether we deserve them or not. However, it is not the case with bad things. We do not accept them and even question the fairness of God. As a matter of fact, if we make a list of good things in life as well as of the bad things, in most cases the former will exceed the latter. By and large, life gives us more compensation and rewards than losses and punishments. If this is the case then it is not fair on our part to doubt the fairness of God.

In order to discuss the subject further, it is necessary to understand the concept of God. We all believe in one or the other form of God whatever we may call Him. After all there is a Supreme Power which is behind all creation and laws of the universe. Movement of terrestrial bodies, creation of day and night, law of gravitation, the changing of weather, falling of rains and scores of such things are all governed by fixed universal laws. Will not there be turmoil and havoc, if there is even slight deviation from these laws ? Even if we do not believe in God in the orthodox sense, we have to believe in the universal laws of nature. For example, if an object is dropped from a height, it has to fall down and it would be foolish to expect it to go up. Even if for argument's sake, it does so, the universe will become so topsy turvy that living will become impossible. Therefore, let us interpret God as a power who governs the laws of the universe which keep things going.

Once we accept this definition of God, we must also accept that there must be certain fixed laws behind good events as well as bad events of life. If we do so, the question of fairness of God, when bad things happen, will not arise. In fact, it would be unfair on our part to expect good things to happen when the laws of nature demand otherwise. Perhaps expecting that would be more disastrous than the consequences of the so-called bad things or seemingly cruel events.

This takes us to the 'Law of karma'. "As we sow, so shall we reap" is an old saying. This is nothing but the 'Law of karma'. Nature expects us to follow certain laws in order to live a healthy, peaceful and harmonious life. How often do we break these laws? The contention is to establish that if we break the laws of nature, why should we not face the consequences? Not only this, nature is quite merciful in the sense that it gives us enough flexibility to break its laws and does not punish, if the laws are broken occasionally. Only when the laws are broken consistently we are punished. If we expect that it should not happen, the laws of nature will lose their meaning. For example, if someone smokes occasionally, he remains almost unaffected by its adverse effects but a chain smoker is bound to suffer whether we wish it or not. In fact, it would be against the law of nature to expect a chain smoker to remain healthy all through his life.

These arguments are very convincing in visible cause and effect cases. However, quite often we suffer in life for no evident cause. It is in such cases that we question the fairness of God. To understand this we have to believe in the theory of rebirth and the continuance of the account of karmas. That is why so many times we suffer for no obvious reasons. The fact is that the cause of suffering is always there, though we may not know it.

However, nature or God is not so cruel so as to leave a suffering person without any hope or remedy. Nature does not make anyone suffer more than his entitlement or capacity to suffer. Even in suffering, there is always a silver lining. When suffering comes, it does not come alone. It comes with wisdom and the strength to face it. In fact, suffering and wisdom are the two sides of the same coin. If so, is this not the kindness of nature? Moreover, no one suffers more than what he deserves. It is like undergoing a term of imprisonment as prescribed in law. The convict is released the day his sentence is over and he no longer remains a convict.

Thus whatever happens to a man is due to his own doings. God or nature does not interfere in this but only ensures that the laws of nature are followed and it does so with a kind heart and may be at times with a heavy heart. We have full freedom of action. No one compels us to do bad karmas. Good karmas bring good things in life while the bad bring bad things. This law of karma is applicable equally to individuals, societies, and nations. If we collectively do bad things, we are also bound to suffer collectively.

The reward or punishment for our karmas may come to us in various forms there being no fixed pattern. Goodness may be returned by nature in the form of good health, good temperament, a good job, promotion, recovery from the disease, a good wife or husband, good children, etc. Similarly, the bad deeds may punish in the form of physical disability, disease, poverty or other bad events. In fact, the 'Law of karma' is the law of effort and destiny. Actions of yesterday constitute the destiny of today and actions of today the destiny of tomorrow. After we are rewarded or punished for an action of ours, its effect is nullified. Some actions produce immediate effect while some are stored for future. These are called 'Sanchit karmas'. Their effect can only be lessened by our present karmas and that is why some people are able to undergo suffering happily as they know that their Sanchit karmas are being nullified and that they can look forward to a brighter period in life.

Fate, destiny, luck etc., are nothing but the effects of 'Sanchit karmas'. They determine the major incidents of our lives, like place of birth, parentage, wealth, children, wife, job, etc. We enjoy the fruits of our good karmas till they are exhausted and unless we store more good karmas, we cannot enjoy them indefinitely. This explains the bad events of life and if we can understand their background, we shall never question the fairness of God. In fact, questioning that will amount to being unfair to God. And if we want God to be fair to us, should we also not be fair to Him ?

- Defeat is a school in which truth always grows strong.
- The tide always comes back. Don't ever accept defeat.
- You must learn to accept defeat without being defeated.
- Good and bad luck are synonymous in a great majority, for instance, for good and bad judgement.
- I am a great believer in luck. The harder I work the more of it I seem to have.
- The ratio between hard work and luck is 70 : 30.

23

LIFE IS A GAME OF TENNIS

Life is compared to so many things and it is advised to take life accordingly. Among these comparisons, life is also compared with game. I feel it is the most appropriate comparison and it means that life is to be played well. Again though the life can be compared with so many games, I consider that life is more like a game of tennis. My consideration may be due to the fact that I played tennis regularly. But I have several points to support my consideration. This is what is going to be discussed in this write-up in order to establish that life is a game of tennis.

Let me first describe briefly the game of tennis. This game is played with a racket and a ball. A net is fixed in the middle of the court touching the ground and the ball is sent across with the help of the racket. There are certain rules of the game. The game is played either in singles or doubles. The objective of playing is to win the game or rather to enjoy the game. In fact, enjoying the game is more important than winning and at times a game won is not enjoyed at all, while a game lost may be much more enjoyable. The same is the case with life. The main objective of life is to enjoy living whether or not we are successful in worldly terms. Here enjoying life is to be taken in a higher sense. Now let us see how the game of tennis teaches us important lessons of life.

The game of tennis begins with a service. One gets two chances for it. One can afford to miss one and not both. If one misses both the chances, the point is lost. Again there can be different approaches to serving. Some players prefer to earn a point through aces. But they have equal chances of losing the point through double faults. My experience is that the chances of earning a point through a mild service are the same or perhaps more than through an ace. An ace may bring applause from the crowd but after an ace, there is no play and the question of enjoying does not arise. Also if such a service is returned, one is generally taken unaware and in all probability the server loses the point. On the other hand, one can always anticipate the return of a mild service and position oneself accordingly. Quite often the opponent takes your mild service so casually that he commits a mistake in the first return itself and gives you a point. My personal experience is that one gets more points through mild services than by hitting aces. The lesson to be learnt is that politeness in life pays more in the long run than harshness. It may appear at times that harshness is bringing success but it is not so in the long run. Moreover, harshness takes away the pleasure of life even in the short run. A harsh word may snap a relationship at once, like an ace, after which there is no game.

The next lesson to be learnt from the 'service' is also very important for life. Some players believe that the first chance of serving is for trial and invariably use the second chance. The result is that they commit double fault quite often. Once you have faltered in serving, there is no question of playing further. At times they commit double fault at such a crucial stage of the game that it becomes suicidal. The lesson to be learnt is that, first of all, one should avoid committing mistakes in life and the opportunity should be grabbed in the first instance itself. If however a mistake has been committed, it should not be repeated because life does not give you many chances. If you miss all your chances, you lose the game of life. Therefore one has to be 'watchful' in order to make use of the opportunities offered by life. In no case should any opportunity be lost in the hope that more opportunities will come. A mistake should only be a genuine failure and not an imposed one.

After the service, the game starts and your objective is to score a point. This happens in two ways: either you commit a mistake or your opponent does. My experience is that one plays best when he plays with a detached attitude. 'Do not pursue victory too hard' is an old proverb and I find it fully applicable in the game of tennis. I have noticed that those who are not prepared to lose, seldom win. The idea is that when one plays with an open mind, his game becomes natural and the chances of his committing mistakes are greatly reduced. And if you do not commit mistake, the chances are that your opponent will and lose the point. This is always an easier way of scoring a point. The lesson to be learnt is that life should be lived as naturally as possible. One should meet life as it comes. This is the surest way of enjoying life even if you do not achieve your worldly goals.

Quite often you come across an opponent who is also like you and does not commit mistakes. You really enjoy the game with such an opponent but after all you want to earn the point. Here comes the capacity of anticipation. One should not only play well but should also be able to anticipate and take positions accordingly. In all probability your opponent will also do the same and you have to counter his anticipation to score a point. In life one comes across such a situation quite often and one has to meet the challenge with intelligence. At times a strategy has to be prepared in advance and far-sightedness is to be shown. Those who fail to do are taken unaware and lose the point.

At times you may not be able to counter anticipation of your opponent. In such a situation you have to take a risk. The stage when risk should be taken is to be decided by intelligence and experience depending upon who your opponent is and what his strengths and weaknesses are. The consideration should be the probability of your winning the point. A calculated risk will bring you a point in most cases. It also makes the game more interesting. In life too, at times it is necessary to take risks but they have to be calculated. Such risks not only bring success but also add to the pleasure of life.

At times you return the ball at such a vulnerable position that your losing the point becomes almost a certainty. In such a situation the best you can do is to face the opponent boldly. This itself makes the opponent commit a blunder, thus giving you a point. And if by chance you are able to return the ball, you are again likely to score a point. Thus by facing the situation boldly you raise the probability of winning a point even in a dismal situation. The same thing is true of life also. In losing moments of life the best thing to do is to face them boldly. In that case the bad moments will greatly lose their hold and may even turn into gains.

As the game proceeds, your stamina becomes a matter of great importance. You may be a very good player but if you are not able to sustain yourself throughout the match, even the initial victory will have no meaning. For this energy has to be optimally used. At times it may be expedient to lose a point or game in order to win the match. In life too, the resources are to be used in an optimum manner. For this at times failures are to be accepted gladly. Those who fail to do so end up becoming laughing stocks while those who do, have the last laugh. Life has to be taken as a whole like a match of tennis. Victory in one or two games or sets has no meaning, if you lose the match. Similarly one has to be victorious in life as a whole.

Lastly it is the satisfaction of playing which matters. At times you enjoy a match greatly even if you lose it. If you have played well, you will always have more satisfaction even if you have lost. So the most important thing is how you play. In life too, it is more important how you live than what you live. The ultimate satisfaction of life comes not from outer possessions but from the inner possessions and only you know that satisfaction. It is a different matter whether the world calls you successful or not.

Thus a game of tennis gives many important lessons for life and if we can adopt them, life itself will become a game of tennis.

24
TIP OF THE ICEBERG

One day I was travelling from Kanpur to New Delhi with a young man and we had discussion on a variety of subjects. The young man had just returned from the USA after doing his MBA and was in the process of settling down in India. The discussion, therefore, focused on this aspect. He had known me for quite sometime and had been seeking my guidance but it was the first opportunity of having such a long session at a stretch. This gave both of us an opportunity to know each other more closely. Perhaps, he was unaware of many aspects of my life, of which he came to know during this journey. At the end of the journey he commented that it had been really a very useful journey and he had got an opportunity of understanding my mind regarding his career planning. To this I lightly remarked that it was only the tip of the iceberg and what had been discussed was only a small portion of what I had in mind. I invited him for further discussion and thereafter we could work out a detailed plan of the activities to be undertaken by him.

Somehow the phrase 'Tip of the Iceberg' got stuck in my mind and I started contemplating over it. I wondered whether the phrase only indicates the application of Archmedes's principle to an ice block floating in the ocean or whether it could be given a deeper meaning. And many interesting comparisons came to my mind which I propose to write here.

My first reaction is that the 'Tip of the Iceberg' is a true description of one's condition in this world. The world is like an ocean and we are like icebergs. Most portion of ours remains submerged in this worldly ocean and only a part remains outside. If we want to know the reality of ourselves, we have to rise above the world. Even if we remain inside the world, we should know our real size. In a way we can say that it is the process of self-realisation which makes us know our identity. And this is possible only when we are able to identify ourselves as different from the objective world.

The 'Tip of the Iceberg' can also be compared to several other aspects of our life. It indicates that we use only part of our talent and most of it remains hidden. We should discover this potential and make use of it. The same concept should be applied to others too. We must understand that like us others too have a lot of hidden potential and they should be motivated to use it. If all of us make full use of our talents, the world will change for the better. Mobilisation of our talent is possible when we become aware of it and make a determined effort to use it.

The comparison with the iceberg should also be used when we look at our shortcomings. Like an iceberg our negative tendencies are not visible to us and if at all we see them, only a part is seen. So the endeavour should be to know our shortcomings and remove them. While there is no need to expose our weaknesses we should gradually overcome them. This is possible only when we are able to accept them.

Another lesson to be learnt from the iceberg is how to float in the ocean of the world. An iceberg floats because the density of the ice is a little less than that of water. It means that though a form of water, an iceberg is different from it. Similarly, while we should be in the world, we should be indifferent to it. This is possible only when we lighten ourselves by not worrying too much about worldly things which in any case are of a transitory nature. If we are able to do so, we can also float in the world like an iceberg and keep our identity intact.

One more lesson to be learnt from the iceberg is that like an iceberg we are also melting away day by day and one day there will be complete merger with the sea. If the vastness of the sea is compared with the vastness of God, we can say that we are from the very beginning part of God and appear to be different for a certain period of time because of the body. Ultimately with the death of the body we merge with God.

Thus the iceberg gives us some very interesting messages about life and if we take them in the right spirit, life can be made much more meaningful and purposeful.

Do something for somebody!

Do something for somebody, somewhere,
while jogging along life's road.
Help someone to carry his burden,
and lighter will grow your load.

Do something for somebody, gladly,
it will sweeten your every care.
In sharing the sorrows of others,
your own are less hard to bear.

Do something for somebody, striving
to help where the way seems long.
And the sorrowful hearts that languish,
cheer up with a little song.

Do something for somebody, always,
whatever may be your creed.
There's nothing on earth that can help you
so much as a kindly deed.

— **Harold Abbott**

25
REFUSE TO BE INSULTED

'Insult' is a word frequently used in day-to-day life. History is full of instances where an 'insult' has turned the course of events and led to major wars. Even the famous war of 'Mahabharata' had its genesis in the 'insult' of Duryodhana by Draupadi. While 'insult' in itself may not be explosive yet it definitely works as a spark and whenever the background is explosive, the spark of insult causes explosion. Quite often the person who is insulted or feels insulted is also the victim of this explosion, while the person who caused it, may remain unaffected. Thus we find that in most of the cases the person feeling insulted suffers more if he allows the explosion to take place. Therefore what should be one's attitude in an insulting situation, deliberate or otherwise? My answer to this question is that you should refuse to be insulted and beat the opponent at his own game. How to do so will be discussed in this write-up.

First of all, one should analyse whether in a given situation one has been insulted or one is only feeling insulted. If we objectively undertake such an analysis, we shall find that in most cases the alleged offender had no intention of insulting us and the events which make us feel insulted are not deliberate acts. They are either on account of someone's ignorance, lack of education, mere innocence, misinformation or our own inferiority complex. In such a situation it is mainly our own ego which makes us feel insulted. There can be a number of such situations. For example, you have been invited to attend a function and you consider yourself important enough to be given a seat in the front row.

When you occupy such a seat, someone points out your mistake. At this you may feel insulted and may even lose your temper. After this even if offered a seat on the dais, you may feel hurt and find it difficult to focus your attention on the deliberations. The right course in such a situation would be to occupy a seat at the back and if you really deserve a front seat, the organisers will probably apologise and offer you a front seat. This will also enhance your prestige in their eyes. However if this does not happen, you may presume that you do not deserve a front seat and by not occupying one, you have saved an ugly situation.

There are a large number of such situations when we feel insulted without being insulted. We do so even with our close relations and friends. An invitation card for an important function at a close friend's place has not reached you and without trying to find out the facts, you start feeling insulted and imputing all sorts of motives to your friend who himself feels sad for your absence from the function. So much so that you even avoid him when he tries to contact you adding to yours as well as his agony. The same thing may happen between brother and brother, father and son or even husband and wife. All such instances indicate your own lack of confidence. A person who is confident of oneself should never react in a hurry but should try to find out the facts. Even if the facts indicate that he has been ignored, he should take them coolly and redefine or review his relationship.

There may be another kind of situation where you have been insulted or ignored deliberately but in good faith. This is done to make you realise something which will help you. A father reprimanding his son, or a teacher punishing his student are such examples. The same thing may be done by a well meaning friend or relative. In such a situation, the role of both becomes important. While the person being insulted or ignored should take it gracefully, the person causing it should also not cross the limit, otherwise the outcome may become counter-productive. However, the underlying message is that there is no cause for feeling insulted. As a matter of fact these situations should refine you and you should be grateful to the person creating such a situation.

Refuse To Be Insulted

The third type of insult is more difficult to deal with and it is when you are insulted deliberately. Such insult may be inflicted out of jealousy, enmity or just to dampen your spirits. The person causing such an insult is likely to be in a superior position than the victim in one way or another. He may be stronger in strength, in position or in wealth. However such persons are internally weak and can be defeated with wisdom. For this the first thing to do is to maintain one's poise. If the poise is lost, the person causing the insult wins the game. Secondly, such a situation should be turned into an opportunity to grow. There are several examples in history where great men became great because they were insulted sometime in their lives but drew deep inspiration from such insults. The example of our own Father of the Nation is known to all of us. An insult by a white man who threw him out of the first class compartment of a running train changed the course of not only his own life but of the whole nation. The situation would perhaps have been different, had he reacted angrily at that moment and ended up in a police lock-up.

Thus we find that in all situations of insult unintentional, in good faith or deliberate, there is no need to feel hurt but every need to think constructively. If we do so, we shall not only elevate ourselves but also win over the person who insults us. In worldly terms we can insult him by refusing to be insulted.

- He who allows himself to be insulted, deserves to be.
- It is often better not to see an insult than to avenge it.
- No one can ever insult you when you know your own worth.
- No one can make you feel inferior without your consent.
- Write injuries in sand, kindness in marble.

26
SWAMI CHINMAYANANDA IN MY LIFE

Sometimes a person or event turns the course of one's life. In my life the turning point was the reading of a book titled *Kindle Life* by Swami Chinmayanandaji. I came across it by chance in November 1980 at Gorakhpur in U.P. Since the background of this incident is interesting, I would like to briefly give the same.

I have been quite sincere and hardworking since my childhood. However, I never knew that these are considered to be the traits of a truly religious person. Religion to me meant observing certain rituals and visiting temples and other religious places. In my childhood I had come across some religious persons who were considered very pious in the village but they never impressed me. The reason was that I had noticed many things wanting in their daily conduct. As a result, I developed an aversion towards the so-called religious people and religious practices.

However, I have always believed in and tried to practise goodness in my life. At times I suffered from the worldly viewpoint but I never thought of giving up goodness. In March 1980, when I got transferred from a very sensitive post at Meerut, a friend of mine commented that good people generally suffer in the later parts of their lives. I was stunned to hear this statement and did not know how to react. But this set me thinking about the rationale behind goodness. I started doubting whether goodness was merely a matter of choice or there was something deeper in it and whether it was essential for one's growth or not.

From Meerut, I came to Lucknow and was posted there for about five months. Thereafter I got transferred to Gorakhpur in the month of August 1980. In October 1980, I came in contact with Shri Deoraha Baba. This contact gave me a lot of peace but not the answer to my doubts. In November 1980, a close friend of mine got engaged and went to Orissa for his marriage. He was living in a single suite of officer's hostel. While leaving Gorakhpur, he had entrusted the setting of his suite to me. Though highly competent and successful in his career, I had always found him a disorganised person and his suite bore testimony to this fact. It took me quite sometime to put his things in order. In doing so, I came across a copy of *Kindle Life*.

I found this book so interesting and convincing that I read it at a single sitting. It gave me a scientific interpretation of religion which established that goodness is an essential part of a religious person. In a way it is a basic qualification for the inner growth of a person. No person can aspire to progress on the higher path without being virtuous. It is like basic qualification for a competitive examination without which one cannot even fill up the application form. I was then convinced about the need for goodness and could follow my path with confidence and conviction. Naturally I also developed a deep reverence for Swami Chinmayanandaji.

Thereafter, I came across a commentary on the Gita by Swamiji. This was presented to me by another friend who had obtained it from Goa while on a training course there. I went through this also over a period of time and found it interesting and convincing. Later, when I had occasion to meet Swamiji personally at Kanpur at Mr B B Gupta's residence on 26 January 1987, Swamiji blessed the book by writing the following words:

"Gita is a Book on Life; and life is NOT a book. Therefore read, reflect, understand and come to live what you appreciate. Thus revise Gita some ten times. See the difference in the texture of your life".
'Love'

Swami Chinmayananda
26 Jan., 1987

Swamiji used to visit Kanpur and Lucknow occasionally. I availed of all the opportunities to meet him. Though I never came very close to him nor attended many of his discourses, I always held him in high esteem and my life was greatly influenced by his writings. Once I had the privilege of inaugurating his 'National Camp' at Pitamah Sadan, Kanpur on 19 February 1989. It was a great joy for me to speak on this occasion. Thereafter, I received a letter from Swamiji.
It reads:

Bombay
26th Feb. 1989

"Thank you for being so nice and cultured in your decorum. In that interior village I was surprised when I came to realise you were an IAS and managing director.
Good of you to bring your wife and son. May Lord's blessing hands be upon you and your family.
Do study three verses a day of Chapter VI, think over the ideas in it. Thus in small quantities complete reading 20 revisions of Chapter VI."
Love

Swami Chinmayananda

After this I visited Pitamah Sadan several times with Shri B B Gupta. Once we decided to visit Sidhbari together and the opportunity came in May 1992. We stayed there for two nights and greatly enjoyed the sublimity of the place. In March 1993, I visited the headquarter of Chinmaya Mission at Bombay. I had a desire to meet Swamiji there but it could not be possible. I remember to have noted down the dates of his visit to Delhi and Kanpur in my diary and looked forward to seeing him at either of these places. Unfortunately, it was not to be so and destiny snatched his body from us in the early hours of 4 August 1993. Of course me and my wife could have the darshan of his mortal remains at Lodhi Road.

Thus a great saint came into my life and changed its course. He must have done so in the lives of millions of other people all over the world. It is impossible to measure the contribution of such personalities towards the welfare of society. They do so not only during their lifetimes but thereafter too. I bow my head in deep gratitude in his memory.

Choose your Words !

A careless word may kindle strife,
A cruel word may wreck a life.

A bitter word may hate instil,
A brutal word may even kill.

A gracious word may smooth the way,
A joyous word may make some life gay.

A timely word may lessen stress,
A loving word may heal and bless.

Tact makes you curb that nasty crack,
When you are on the brink.
It's really thinking all you say,
Not saying all you think !

27
THE HEAT IS WITHIN US

In November 1993, I was appointed an observer of the Election Commission for the Himachal Pradesh Assembly elections. The duty was in Mandi District. I had to go there three times. For going there I used to fly to Kullu from Delhi and then drive by road. The first visit was a short one, during my second visit I toured the Mandi District extensively as it was during the polling period. The third visit was during the period of counting towards the end of November. Since no trouble was expected during counting, I decided to stay at Manali for a day during the last visit. Being the end of November, the place had become quite cold by that time. There was one more officer staying at Manali, who was also an observer of the commission.

I was alone during this visit and it was quite cold. After a walk about the town, I returned to the Circuit House in the evening and took to reading. After dinner, I had a long chat with the other officer who had been a keen student of history. He told me several things which I was eager to know. Thereafter I went to sleep. By that time, it had become very cold.

In the inspection houses of Himachal Pradesh, quite thick quilts are provided in addition to blankets. They are also maintained well, particularly those in the VIP rooms. I am normally not in the habit of using a room-heater during winters as I cannot sleep while the heater is on. Since good quilts were provided, I went to bed after putting off the heater and had a very sound sleep. As usual I woke up in the morning at about 6.00 a.m.

While waiting for bed-tea, a feeling of gratitude towards the quilt came to my mind which kept me warm in such a cold weather. Also came to my mind the scientific analysis of this warmth. I thought about the source of the heat and arrived at the conclusion that it was my own body's heat which had kept me warm. The quilt provided the warmth by merely stopping it from dissipating. It had no role except that of an insulator. From this I derived a very important lesson in life. I thought that if just by insulating the body, I could keep my body warm in such a cold weather, it should be possible to face any adverse situation in life by insulating myself from it. However insulations may be of different types. At times we may have to insulate from bad company, bad thoughts, worldly pleasures and similar other things. The idea is to convey that the potential to face any situation lies within us only. External supports are only tools and if we can use them properly, we can face all situations. In a nutshell, we can say that the heat is within us, we have to protect it from dissipating.

Perseverance

Genius, that power which dazzles mortal eyes,
Is off but perseverance in disguise.
Continuous efforts, itself, implies,
In spite of countless falls, the power to rise.
Twixt failure and success, the point's so fine,
Men sometimes know not, when they touch the line.
Just when the pearl was waiting one more plunge,
How many a struggler has thrown up the sponge !

— Edward Hale

28
HAPPY NEW YEAR

Every year starts with the adjectives of 'happy' and 'new'. By the time it comes to an end both the adjectives are dropped and it simply becomes a year to be buried in the grave of time. We all wish each other, saying "Happy New Year," send greeting cards, make telephone calls, spend evenings in expensive restaurants, eating, drinking and dancing. These are different ways of celebrating the new year. I too send greetings to a large number of friends and well-wishers but instead of spending the evening out, I prefer to stay at home and spend the evening in my usual manner. I even find it difficult to remain awake till midnight, as it disturbs my next day's routine. However, I cannot stop my sleep getting disturbed as soon as it is midnight, due to the sudden explosion of crackers in the neighbourhood. This is how my so-called 'Happy New Year' begins.

Once I made some philosophical analysis of the whole concept of a 'Happy New Year'. After all, what kind of change does a new year bring? Physically there appears to be no change anywhere when the new year arrives. Everything keeps going on in the same manner as before. Time is something continuous and man has drawn boundaries only for the sake of convenience. Of course, these boundaries are related to certain physical phenomena like rotation of the earth around the sun or rotation of the moon around the earth. Thus in one calendar year, the earth completes one round of the sun. In this sense the year definitely has a boundary but it is hardly perceptible to the common man and I don't think he cares about it.

Einstein's theory of relativity adds a very interesting dimension to the concept of time. In a nutshell, it says there is nothing absolute about the past, the present and the future. The past for 'A' may be the present for 'B' and so on. For example, when we see a star in the sky, for us it is its present condition or situation whereas in reality it is its past condition or situation. There are stars from which light reaches us after several million years and even the nearest star becomes visible after about four years. This makes the whole concept of the new year or the past year irrelevant.

You may wonder what am I trying to convey. I am aware of this and am trying to arrive at some meaningful conclusions. By adding these dimensions, I only wish to convey that most of us have a very narrow view of the so-called 'Happy New Year.' While there is no harm in celebrating it the way most of us do, a little more reflection will not only add to our pleasure of celebration but also make it more meaningful. Here are a few points for reflection at the time of the 'Happy New Year'.

a) First of all, the new year is an occasion to review our performance in the year gone by. We should derive satisfaction from our achievements and lessons from our failures.

b) The new year is a time to think of our friends and well-wishers. During the year some of them may have changed places. Even our addresses may have changed. This is an occasion to update our information about them and help them to update theirs. It provides a wonderful opportunity to get in touch with each other.

c) A list of those whom we want to wish a "Happy New Year" should be prepared with complete addresses and greetings should be conveyed well in time. It should not matter whether these are reciprocated or not. In case of continuous default, the list may be modified in the subsequent years. Any lapses due to oversight should be taken care of at the earliest.

d) When we wish others "Happy New Year", we should mean it, even if we do so in formality. This will increase our compassion and enrich us.

e) We must use discrimination in conveying our wishes. There may be friends/relatives who are in trouble and in all probability the new year may not be a happy one for them. In such cases, a casual wish has no meaning. It may even hurt them. We have to show our real concern for them so as to give them strength to face their troubles. We must also pray for this strength.

f) And, lastly, we must contemplate over the fact that each 'Happy New Year' is shortening our life. The time available to us to achieve our objectives is reduced by one year. We must therefore redefine our goals, if necessary refix our priorities. This will help us in using our energy more efficiently making the achievement of goal easier.

By following these suggestions we shall not only make the new year, happy but the whole life new and happy.

The Treasures of Time
Yesterday is
a Cancelled Cheque ....
Tomorrow is
a Promissory Note .....
Today is
Ready Cash ...... use it !

29
SPIRITUAL INVESTMENT

Prices of land have zoomed over the past ten or twenty years. The rise is mind-boggling in towns like Delhi. Those who did not buy land earlier can hardly dream of doing so now. Those who did, have a great sense of relief and consider themselves very fortunate.

An opportunity to buy land near Delhi came in my life too. In 1980, I was posted at Lucknow as deputy secretary in the Industries Department. At that time the new township of Noida was coming up on the outskirts of Delhi and was considered a profitable place for investment. At that time the mad rush for real estate had not begun and so it was almost a buyer's market. The chief executive officer of Noida was an IAS officer who had been my Collector when I was a Senior district magistrate. Once he had come to Lucknow for a meeting and came to my office and offered me a plot of land at a prime location in Noida. The offer did not attract me much and I declined it. Today prices of land there have gone up so high that I regret my decision of declining the above offer. Of course, I got another opportunity to buy land in Lucknow and I have constructed a modest house there.

While I missed the opportunity of investing in land in 1980, a great turn came in my life. Soon after I was transferred to Gorakhpur where I came across some great saints as well as books. My association with them changed the course of my life which became much more meaningful to me. I could understand the true purpose of living and started acquiring the qualities necessary to achieve it. Once on this path, I started feeling contentment in all walks of life and all petty temptations were overcome. With steady progress in this direction, I began enjoying every bit of life. It does not mean that there are no troubles in my life. In fact, there are more than what I would consider my legitimate share, but with inner strength, I am able to accept them without fretting and fuming. Very few, I am afraid, are able to appreciate this aspect of my life. For most people, material success is the only measure of life.

Let us compare the two investments. Investment in material things brings us respect and security. It takes care of our old age and provides us an opportunity to help others. It keeps our children happy and we can also provide them a good future. The positive aspect of material prosperity cannot be denied. But it has a negative aspect also. Quite often we forget to draw the line and fall into a vicious circle. If so, we miss the finer aspects of life while the negative aspect of material progress soon starts troubling us. The only way to counter the negative aspect is the finer or, say, the spiritual aspect of life. Thus a balanced growth of both aspects of life is necessary in order to live a purposeful life.

There is a tendency on the part of most of us to keep postponing our spiritual growth. We consider it something which can be acquired in old age. But the fact is that like material growth, spiritual growth also requires an alertness of our faculties. It is something which needs an intelligent understanding of life and if we do not show an inclination at the right time, it may be too late. Moreover no one can be sure of old age. It may or may not come. Even if it comes, it may come with such handicaps that, understanding the spiritual aspect of life may not be possible. We then end up saying that we did not invest in spirituality when the opportunity came and now it is beyond our capacity. This establishes the necessity of spiritual investment at the right time.

It may be argued that if nothing goes wrong in life then what is the necessity of growing spiritually? After all, such growth is required for bad times only. Against this there are two arguments. First, that no one can be sure of having good times only. In every one's life, there come difficult situations. For facing such situations, we need inner strength which only comes from spiritual growth. Secondly, it is not true to say that inner growth is required only in times of adversity. It is equally required in the time of prosperity. One needs inner growth to face prosperity in a dignified manner. Moreover, in prosperity we can develop our spiritual dimension so as to face adversity in a dignified manner. Thus the spiritual growth is required for good as well as bad times.

We can also compare our spiritual growth with defence forces. Many may question the desirability of maintaining strong defence forces at a time when the prospects of war are receding. But they forget that this is mainly due to the presence of a strong army. Only powerful nations can talk of peace. Moreover, defence forces have a role in peace-time also. Without peace-time they cannot prepare themselves for war-times. Similarly, without growing spiritually during prosperity we cannot face adversity in a dignified manner. And if we achieve enough spiritual growth during good times there would perhaps be no such thing as bad times.

We may, therefore, conclude by saying that timely spiritual investment is as necessary as timely material investment. Once we miss the opportunity to do so, it may be too late.

- He who gives man spiritual knowledge, is the greatest benefactor of mankind.
- Indifference to worldly pleasures is the chief requisite for spiritual advancement.

30

WE DO NOT NEED A GUN

I was district magistrate of Basti in Uttar Pradesh during the year 1982-84. At that time it had not been bifurcated and was the biggest district of Uttar Pradesh in terms of rural population. At the same time it was one of the most backward districts and bad from the law and order point of view. Therefore, for a person to carry a gun was considered a measure of safety as well as prestige. A large number of applications for gun licences were always pending with the district magistrate. I tried to streamline the system of granting licences and ensured that these were issued only in deserving cases.

One day I was sitting in my office in a somewhat relaxed mood when one such aspirant came to see me. I knew him as he was a respected person of the town. For sometime he talked about general things and thereafter came to the subject of law and order. His complaint was that the number of guns in the district was increasing and the sight of so many gun-carrying persons created fear among the common people. He also wondered that if everyone would carry a gun, how would the situation of law and order improve?

These words of his gave me a very pleasant surprise as it was very rare that someone in that district would talk against the number of guns and particularly an aspirant of the gun. I got impressed as well as interested and wanted to discuss the matter further hoping that some solution to the problem might come from him. I agreed with him and asked him to suggest some solution to the problem created by the increasing number of arms.

And prompt came the reply that a gun be given to him also. He said this very innocently without realising that the solution suggested by him would only add to the problem instead of solving it. I could, however, convince him that he did not require a gun for safety and he did not press for a licence as long as I was the district magistrate.

This incident fascinated me so much that I have narrated it a number of times to various people. I see a great similarity in the different aspects of human life today and this incident. Be it the matter of indiscipline, corruption, dowry, nepotism, exploitation of weaker sections or any other evil, most of us believe in the kind of solution suggested by the above gentleman. We see corruption in society, also feel bad about it but when it comes to doing something about it, we feel that our indulgence also is the answer. Similar is the case with other evils. We forget that by doing so we add to the evil instead of removing it. Everyone feels bad about the dowry system except when it applies to oneself. We talk of the sincerity, discipline, etc., only as long as it is not demanded from us. The result is the chaos we see around in all walks of life. A situation has reached where we cause suffering to each other and feel that the remedy lies in doing so only.

At this moment a small story comes to my mind. Once God appointed a commission to study the difference in the conditions prevailing in hell and heaven. The commission decided to go to hell first. It found it to be an excellent place, well built and prosperous. There was plenty to eat and drink. However, the commission observed that the inhabitants were very weak and kept quarrelling among themselves all the time. The reason was that they were unable to bend their elbows and therefore could not take the food up to their mouths, though it was available in plenty. Starved of food, they had become very weak and irritable making them quarrel with each other. Overall the scene was very pathetic and all the inhabitants were helpless not knowing what to do.

Thereafter the commission visited heaven. It found similar conditions there also. The place was well built and there was plenty to eat and drink. Again the inhabitants were unable to bend their elbows but they were healthy and cheerful. On close observation, it was found that, though each one of them was unable to take the food up to his mouth, he was doing so for others and thus each one was being fed by others. The result was obvious with everyone enjoying the prosperity of the place.

The same story is applicable to our society also. It is up to us whether we create a heaven by helping each other or a hell by thinking of ourselves only. In both cases the effect is in geometrical progression. In the first case it is elevating and in the second one it is depressing. While some negative elements will always exist in society, these are to be dealt with suitably, through the administrative process. The trouble arises when the overall situation becomes negative. This is what appears to have happened in present times. This trend has to be reversed and it does not require any, great ideas. The only change called for is a change of attitude. Instead of thinking of only ourselves, if we think of others too, the whole society will be benefited. An individual will also then stand to gain as a member of the society.

Fortunately, such a sorry state of affairs does not exist everywhere. There are many positive examples. There are many instances where great results have been achieved as a result of mutual cooperation. There are villages where there is no dispute, no need to lock houses, no lack of resources, etc. At such places, life is almost heavenly. There are also organisations where ideal working conditions prevail and people work in mutual trust and enjoy the fruits of the same. However, such cases are exceptional but they demonstrate the efficacy of the concept.

The idea is to convey that when we talk of the evils prevalent in the society, we should try to understand whom are we addressing. It is futile to expect solutions from others as they too are victims of the evils. To think of a solution by following the rat race only adds to the problem. In fact, the problem should be addressed to oneself and a solution found within. Instead of thinking what one can do for oneself, one should think what he can do for others. In a way this approach is more selfish because ultimately the benefits will be reaped by him only and these would be much more than what one can gain by thinking of oneself only. If all of us do so, life will become heavenly and none of us will need a gun.

> I expect to pass
> through life but once !
> If therefore,
> there by any kindness
> I can show,
> or any good thing
> I can do to any fellow being ....
> Let me do it now,
> and not defer or neglect it,
> as I shall not pass
> this way again !
>
> *William Penn*

31

THE GANGES DOES NOT HOARD

Once I got the opportunity of visiting Haridwar twice in quick succession. I enjoyed both the visits immensely. The sight of a large number of pilgrims having a bath at 'Hari Ki Pauri' and participating in the evening *aarti* fascinated me. The faith of our people always leaves a great impression on me whenever I visit a holy place. Irrespective of reasoning behind this faith, I believe that in it lies the strength of our people. It is a different matter that this faith is exploited by some.

I do not have any craving for taking bath in the Ganges. Somehow it has always been so. Perhaps, it is an impression of my childhood when I observed some so-called holy women of my village behaving in a very unholy manner and their holiness being attributed to their frequent Ganges baths. That was, perhaps, why I never cared to bathe in the Ganges during my 15 days camp on the bank of the river as person in charge of the *Kartika Mela* in the early years of my service. Even during the above two visits, I took bath in the Ganges only once and that too not at 'Hari Ki Pauri'.

However, there was a vast difference between my last visit and these two visits after a gap of almost ten years. A lot of water had flown down the river since then and a lot of wisdom had dawned on me. Questioning the faith of people is no more my nature though I may not have the same faith. I feel faith and reason are two different things and it is not wise to apply reason in matters of faith. A faith may or may not be inspired by reason, but true faith is always enriching. At times it is beyond reason.

With this change in my outlook, the visit to the town of holy Ganges was very enjoyable and elevating. I keenly observed the flowing river and wondered at the service it has rendered to the people from time immemorial. While thinking thus, I was fascinated by the scheme of Mother Nature which ensures that there is always a steady flow of water in the Ganges. In fact, the holiness of the Ganges is due to its flow. The moment it stops flowing, its whole sanctity will be lost. It does not consider it necessary to hoard its water in fear of the future. Even then, no one can say for how long the Ganges has been flowing and will continue to flow. Mother Nature takes care of it on its own.

There is a great lesson to learn from this fact. It applies to our acquisitions too. The moment we start hoarding our acquisitions, unholiness creeps in and they become putrefied. The acquisition then becomes a liability instead of an asset. Be it money, knowledge or any other acquisition, their flow should continue for the benefit of the society at large. The moment we try to store them for our use only, their sanctity is lost. In that case they cease to serve any good even to ourselves, leave alone society. Thus even the virtues become the sources of nuisance, when not shared properly.

The example of the holy Ganges should also take away any fear that we may have of replenishing our resources. If Mother Nature can replenish the mighty river like the Ganges for time immemorial, it can always meet our needs. These will always be taken care of provided we are willing to share what we have. In fact, when we show our willingness to share, others too come forward to share what they have. Like the holy Ganges which grows bigger and bigger as it flows and ultimately becomes one with the ocean, our virtues too grow by sharing. We then merge with the Creator which is the ultimate aim of life.

So the simple lesson to be learnt is that all our acquisitions come from Mother Nature and we have no exclusive right to them. They are to be shared and not to be hoarded. If we do so, we too can become as holy as the Ganges.

> What we have is a gift from Him.
> What we do with what we have is our gift to Him.

32

HOW LUCKY WE ARE

In April 1990, I was nominated for a twelve-week training programme in U.K. under the Colombo Plan. The course was to be held at Ilkley near Leeds, a small town with a population of about 20,000. However, it had all the amenities of a big town like good market, parks, schools, clubs, etc. The town was quite prosperous going by the number of cars. Overall it was a lovely place and life seemed quite comfortable.

In the same course there was another officer from the Kerala cadre. He was a year junior to me. We became quite friendly very soon. During the first week, one day we were walking on the streets of Ilkley, appreciating its beauty and comforts. Spontaneously came from my friend, "How lucky they are!" Though he was right yet his way of saying implied as if we were unlucky. So I kept silently thinking it to be the best way of responding. He felt little uneasy with my silence and wanted to know the reason. I said I would agree with him if he maintained his opinion till the end of the course. The matter ended there.

As days passed by, we became closer to each other. We had many things in common. We both were North Indians and vegetarians. We used to cook our dinner together. Soon we started learning about the weaker side of the so-called heavenly materialistic life of Western society. Our first experience was in the matter of food. Being vegetarian we found it very difficult to manage our food, particularly the lunch, which we had to take in the mess. The problem was on two counts. Firstly, very few vegetarian dishes were available and, secondly, they were so mixed up with non-vegetarian dishes that the sight of them repelled us. My own problem was compounded by my being diabetic. Our request to provide us something which we could eat without reservation, brought no result. My case was referred to a dietician whose report didn't come till the end of the course. As a result I had to stop taking lunch in the mess and managed on my own. At times we tried to draw the attention of the Course Director by appealing to his emotions but there was no effect. Every time some rule or management problem was made an excuse.

This set us thinking about our own society and the country. Howsoever poor we may be, we cannot see others going hungry, more so if they happen to be our guests. Nothing to say of human beings, even dumb animals are taken care of in our country. Most of us derive a great sense of pleasure from feeding others. I don't think that if a foreign national in our land poses a genuine problem we would not do our best to help him, particularly in matters of food. But what we experienced in U.K. was just the opposite. For our course director, everything was commercial matter and genuine human need was no consideration. This made my friend doubt his opinion expressed in the beginning of the course.

In the course of our interaction with several natives, we learnt about many other strengths of our society. The first, of course, was that we are much better hosts. We take care of our guests even at the cost of our own convenience. Secondly, our family system is a matter of envy to them. It is difficult for them to imagine how a marital bond can last throughout one's life. When we were to return at the end of the course to join our families, some native lightly remarked that as far as they were concerned, one could not be sure of finding his family intact after a gap of so much time. This could be an exaggeration but it definitely reflected the insecurity of their family system. Through another incident we learnt that doctors in U.K. do not attend to patients during weekends. Those who can be approached are very expensive. As a result, a patient has to wait till the next working day, irrespective of his problem. Similarly, meeting someone without an appointment is almost impossible. As a result the problem of loneliness is increasing causing many complications. All this is not to suggest that nothing is good in Western society. There are plenty of things to be learnt from it. The idea is not to compare the two societies, but is to establish that it is wrong to pass a hasty value judgement on any society. Every society has its strengths and weaknesses. Also a strength from one point of view may be a weakness from another. Indian society has plenty of strengths but we are becoming unaware of them. On the other hand we try to adopt the weaknesses of other societies. This had made my friend to comment in the beginning. However, having observed things closely, he changed his remark from "How lucky they are!" to "How lucky we are!". My silence in the beginning was also understood by him.

- Crystals, carpets and chandeliers make a nice house but only the smiles on the faces of the resident make it a home.
- East or west, home is best.
- Every home is a university and the parents are the teachers.
- He is the happiest, be he king or peasant, who finds peace in his home.
- What's the good of a home if you are never in it?
- The first indication of domestic happiness is the love of one's home.

33
BRAKES OF THE LIFE VEHICLE

In Lucknow, there is a 'Literacy House', an institution which has done very good work in the field of adult education. Many years back I became quite friendly with its director and used to meet him on my way to Lucknow from Kanpur. He was a retired civil servant who served the institution with dedication for a long time. However, towards the end of his tenure, he appeared to be quite upset with the state of affairs in the institution. Moreover, he had some serious personal problems. One day when I met him, he was in a sad mood. He was glad to see me and shared his problems with me. We started thinking why difficulties come in life and whether there are any positive aspects of them. Instantly a few ideas came to my mind which I am sharing here.

Normally, we consider the difficulties of life as something negative and retarding. We feel that they check the progress of life and delay our reaching the destination. We refuse to see any blessing in them and curse either God or the person who seemingly caused them or ourselves for our past karma. At times our cursing may be justified too but that leads us nowhere. In fact the process of cursing itself consumes a lot of our energy and thus further delays our destination. What then should be our attitude towards the difficulties?

Let us take two examples. Think of an aeroplane landing on the ground. When it lands, its speed is quite high which has to be brought down fast. For this the dampers are opened which resist the movement of the plane. Obviously it is a negative role which delays the reaching of the aeroplane to its destination. But this delay is something desirable and positive. If the speed is not reduced the aeroplane will perhaps never reach its destination and so also the passengers. Now consider a parachute landing. When one jumps with a parachute, it opens and reduces the speed of falling. If this does not happen, the person will fall under gravity and the consequences are obvious. Here also the role of the parachute is seemingly negative, that is, dampening the speed. Obviously none of us consider so and here, also dampening is something desirable in order to reach the destination safely.

These two examples will perhaps indicate the message which is being tried to be conveyed. If we look at life's difficulties with this attitude, we shall understand their utility and consider them helpful in reaching our target. The precaution to be taken is that they should not dampen our spirit so much that the movement is stopped altogether. In that case one will never reach one's destination. It is, therefore, necessary that the propelling force should be greater than the dampening force. Then only will the resultant movement be forward. The difficulties also provide us time for introspection without which one may follow a wrong path and never reach the destination. Thus they act as navigating aids in the voyage of life.

If we compare life with a road vehicle, the role of difficulties becomes all the more meaningful. A vehicle is a device which runs on account of friction between its wheels and the road. And what is friction? Is it not something negative in the ordinary parlance? However, without friction the movement of the vehicle is not possible. Then consider the brakes of a vehicle. What is their role? Is it not negative which retards the vehicle? But will anyone accept a vehicle without brakes? The role of the brakes in a vehicle is as important as that of the engine and the accelerator. In one sense brakes are more important because their failure may prevent you from ever reaching the destination while the engine failure or low speed may only delay it. That is why while driving we generally find on the road sides a warning "Better late than never".

Thus life's difficulties are like a vehicle's brakes. A life without difficulties is like a vehicle without brakes. Howsoever expensive and beautiful a vehicle may be, it is useless without brakes. Of course, here too the precaution is that the motivation for living should be more than the dampening by difficulties. Then only the movement will be forward and one can aspire to reach the goal safely.

A word of clarification in the end is necessary. There are two kinds of difficulties. Some are caused by God or, say, by nature and some are created by us. In fact, the latter are much more than the former. The above discussion is applicable to the difficulties created by nature in the path of a well meaning sincere person. It may or may not apply in case of self-created difficulties. The distinction between the two may be summed up in this manner: "Difficulties created by God are few and for a purpose, while the difficulties created by us are many and without any purpose".

It is the God created difficulties which are the brakes of the life vehicle.

- Every stone can be a stepping stone.
- Man has a hidden treasure within, difficulties and setbacks bring it forth.
- The first and last thing you have to do in this world is to last in it and not be smashed by it.

34
WHOM DO WE ADDRESS TO

After taking over as development commissioner (Iron and Steel) at Calcutta in July 1994, I paid a brief visit to Madras on my way to Trichur. On my return also I stayed at Madras for a day. I had flown from Calcutta to Madras and from Madras to Calcutta by Indian Airlines. Incidentally both the flights caused some anxiety and incovenience. The flight to Madras took off from Calcutta almost in time but as soon as the plane was airborne, the captain declared that it had developed a technical problem and landed back at Calcutta. There was no immediate announcement of the alternate arrangement by the Airlines. I was to catch a train from Madras to Trichur in the evening and it was already noon at Calcutta. While all the passengers became anxious, I was all the more so. However, I was sure that some alternative would come soon and fortunately it did. Contrary to expectations, an alternate plane was arranged by Indian Airlines and we again left Calcutta at about 1300 hours so as to reach Madras in time. As a result, I could attend to some of my official duties as well as comfortably catch the train for Trichur.

On my way back, initially the flight was announced to be on time. The passengers passed through the security check and were waiting in the lounge for boarding announcement. However, after some time an announcement was made about the plane having developed some technical problem and the consequent delay. The passengers were advised to come out of the lounge, get new boarding passes and also some refreshment from the snacks-counter. The flight was a late evening flight and this delay made it very inconvenient. Naturally the passengers were very upset at this announcement and reluctantly left the lounge to follow the instructions. I too felt the same way but within I was keeping my cool. After going through the drill of surrendering boarding passes and getting new ones, we stood in a queue for light refreshments. We were expecting something better to be served so as to partially take care of our annoyance but what we were given only added to it. On a big paper plate there were two small biscuits along with the choice of a cup of tea, coffee or cold drink. There was visible annoyance on the faces of all the beneficiaries of this hospitality and the ripples were widening in the queue also. So much so that one of the passengers standing in the queue lost his temper and started abusing not only the Indian Airlines but the whole of India. Of course, most of us were doing so silently. He appealed to a co-passenger to take him to a good city restaurant so that he could eat something better. However, it was not feasible at that time but anyway, he refused to accept the snacks offered by the airline. I watched all this with amusement and in the process got a better deal from the counter staff who gave the share of such passengers to others. Overall I did not dislike the refreshment as I was quite hungry. Fortunately soon the plane was declared to be fit and our hopes of reaching home the same night revived.

Well, the point I am making here is about the outburst of the gentleman in the queue at Madras airport. Such outbursts are not uncommon. We come across such incidents almost daily. Only the victim and the target of the outburst vary. If such outbursts are carefully analysed, one would come to the conclusion that we all are victims of one another. 'A' may curse 'B', 'B' may curse 'C' and 'C' may curse 'A'. The net result is that sometimes we are victims and sometimes the cause of such outbursts. We forget that after all the quality of human beings in a given set-up is the same and that we ourselves are no better than others. If we are not prepared to see any faults in us and remove them, what right do we have to expect perfectness from others? In such situations, it is very difficult to understand to whom we should address our outburst.

I am not saying that inefficiency or bad service should be accepted. By all means it should be resisted and resisted forcefully. But mere cursing does not help. In all probability such outbursts make the system worse. The right approach would be to understand the situation coolly and if found that it has arisen as a result of wilful neglect or callousness on the part of an individual or system, the same should be dealt with in an effective manner. That way we will not only save ourselves from agony and anger but will render a service to the system as well as to other possible victims. In short, the problem should be addressed to a definite target, and not in the air which helps no one.

The second lesson to be learnt from such events is to consider whether we ourselves are not a cause of such situations, when it comes to our dealing with others. As a matter of fact, this is a better way of addressing the problem and, if all of us do so, there will be no occasion for situations which upset us. We may also be a cause of such situations and if others cause so much agony to us, why should we not avoid such situations? This approach will not only help individuals but also the system.

Thus, whenever a situation upsets us, the problem should not only be addressed to the relevant authorities with an objective mind, it should also be addressed to oneself. But most of us do not do ; and thus add to the problem instead of solving it. No wonder, we increasingly face such situations and make our lives more miserable. Let us, therefore, approach problems with an objective mind. After all the purpose of all progress is to feel more peaceful. But if instead of feeling peaceful, we feel upset and anxious like the friend at Madras airport, the purpose of the progress is lost. In all probability he was a successful person in life but that success became the source of his trouble because he did not address the problem correctly.

So next time you come across a situation which upsets you, remember to address it correctly. That way you will help yourself as well as the system.

- Introspection is the best prescription for happiness.
- When we have not what we like, we must like what we have.

35
LIFE AND THE RUBIK CUBE

Some years back the rubik cube came out as a popular and interesting game. It is a cuboid with six faces of six different colours. Each face consists of nine squares and each square can be rotated on two different axes. The game involves rotating of these squares in such a manner that each face of the cuboid becomes a single colour. Overall it is a complex exercise and most players fail to achieve the desired result. However, many have acquired such a skill that they can achieve the desired result in a surprisingly short time. It is a beautiful sight to see the six faces of six different colours presenting a harmonious look. Some books have also been written on this game and shows held to demonstrate it. I myself however never got much interested in the game and therefore did not often play it.

Once I had gone to Trichur on the occasion of Guru Poornima. In the evening I was on a walk with another devotee who is settled in Muscat. He told me about the craze for this game in certain countries and how some of the players had acquired a great skill in it. And then we started comparing life with the game of rubik cube. We felt that life too was as complicated as the rubik game and that it was a question of acquiring a skill in living if we wanted to make it harmonious. In the rubik game, as one proceeds, one finds that despite one's best efforts different colours intrude and it becomes almost impossible to bring the same colours on all the six faces. Some are able to achieve success on one and some on two or three faces. Very rarely does one find a player who can restore all the faces to a single colour.

In life too, as we proceed to achieve harmony, some event or the other breaks it and we have to start afresh. It is only after we have learnt the art of living that such events do not disturb us but in a way make life more interesting and challenging. With the growth of wisdom, the time taken to accept these events gets reduced further and further. Thereafter, all events of life are accepted in a very natural manner. Eventually one becomes like those players of the rubik cube who reach the six-face stage within a very short time. For such people life becomes harmonious and nothing can disturb them. Such persons are the yogis in the true sense.

Reaching such a state of harmony is the ultimate purpose of life. For this one has to understand the principles of life, believe in them and practise them. There is no short-cut to it. However, once this skill is acquired, no one can take it away from you. You will then be able to play with life in the same way as a skilled person plays with the rubik cube, notwithstanding its complex nature.

- Always remember ! No one can make you unhappy without your consent.
- What we really need is head and heart combined. And that is harmony.

36
REFUSE TO DISLIKE

Once I went on an official tour to Assam and Meghalaya. In Shillong my colleague and I had some spare time and so we decided to drive upto Cherrapunji. The drive was very beautiful and we came across some rare natural beauty on the way. We ate our packed lunch on the way, sitting on a parapet wall on the roadside. The sight of the hillock on the opposite side was superb. So much so that despite being a steelman, I started thinking how beautiful the earth would have been without any steel. Anyway it was a momentary thought and after sometime we drove further.

At Cherrapunji we sat in a small restaurant, looking at the surroundings and tasting some local sweets. There we met a person who must have been in his fifties. By his looks and expression, he appeared to be an educated man hailing from North India. Perhaps he was the owner of or a frequent visitor to the restaurant. When asked he told us that he was from Punjab. One of our colleagues asked him how he had decided to settle down in Cherrapunji and how he liked the place. He did not like being asked all these questions saying these were personal matters and required a long time to explain. However, he told that he had retired from the BSF and most of his family members were settled in Canada. Since he did not like going there, he decided to stay back at Cherrapunji. He also said that he did not dislike anything except dishonesty and fraud. Though he did not hold a very good opinion about the locals, on the whole he liked the place.

This attitude of the man impressed me a lot. Obviously the matter was not so simple. He must have had deep wounds within him. Yet he had adopted a positive approach to life by refusing to dislike his environment. While driving back to Shillong we talked about him and we all appreciated his attitude. The whole thing set me thinking that there was a great lesson to be learnt from him. I, myself, believe in the same approach to life. When I decided to come to Calcutta, many friends and well-wishers asked me whether I liked the place. My answer had always been that I had never thought of disliking the place. And believe me I meant it too. I do not mean to say that there is nothing to dislike in Calcutta. In fact, there is plenty but what is the point in dwelling upon them ? One can always identify so many likable things in any given situation and need not pay attention to others. If one can adopt this approach to life, life becomes much more beautiful.

To be fair in my assessment of the person we met at Cherrapunji, I would say that though he was apparently happy, there appeared to be some bitterness within him. That is why he did not like being asked about his personal life. This dislike was against his claim that he did not dislike anything. He also said that he did not like dishonesty and fraud. While he was correct from a worldly point of view, going a little deeper would reveal that even this dislike is negative. While things like dishonesty, fraud, ugliness, etc., are to be opposed, there is no point in disliking them. The thought of disliking adversely affects us and creates disharmony. This way we become the victim for no fault of ours. It is like saying, "Hate the sin, not the sinner." If we follow this advice, peace will never be lost.

There is one more way of looking at things. The whole creation of God consists of opposites. In fact, without opposites, there will be no existence. For example, we can talk of the good only so long the bad also exists. Similarly, there is no meaning of pleasure without pain. This logic can also be extended to all other things. Beauty has to coexist with ugliness. Piousness is to coexist with wickedness. Honesty is to coexist with dishonesty, so on and so forth. If we accept this fact of life, we have no reason to dislike anything. All things have to be accepted as they are. The only freedom we have is to play our own role in the best possible way in given circumstances.

Whatever way we approach, there is no point in our disliking a situation and by refusing to dislike it we can turn every situation into something we like.

Home is where there's one to love us !

Home is not merely four square walls,
Though with pictures hung and gilded.
Home is where, affection calls,
Filled with shrines the heart has builded !

Home ! Go watch the faithful dove,
Sailing beneath the heaven above us.
Home is where, there's one to love !
Home is where, there's one to love us !

Home is not merely roof and room,
It needs something to endear it.
Home is where, the heart can bloom,
Where there's some kind lip to cheer it !

What is home with none to meet,
None to welcome, none to greet us?
Home is sweet and only sweet
Where there's one, we love to meet us !

— **Charles Swain**

37

WHY SHOULD YOU QUIT?

The incident relates to November 1978. I was posted as the additional district magistrate (Development) of Meerut and also the chief executive officer of Zila Parishad. In that month a mela used to be organised at Garh Mukteshwar on the occasion of *Kartika Poornima*. The site of the mela was on the banks of the Ganges where a small township used to come up. People came to the mela in large numbers, most of them from rural areas. They mostly came on bullock carts with great devotion.

As CEO of the Zila Parishad, I was to look after the arrangements at the mela. For this purpose the district magistrate, who was the chairman of the Zila Parishad, had delegated all his powers to me. I planned everything meticulously and everything started off well. My effort was to put the available resources to optimum use. Naturally, this required some cuts in the expenditure incurred on the members of the mela committee. At the same time, I decided to give some more facilities to the staff who had to work hard during the mela. I also observed that more complaints came from the members themselves rather than the public who accepted everything in the name of Ganga maa. The nature of complaints from the members was more personal than of public interest.

The mela committee used to meet periodically in the evening under my chairmanship. I was then a young officer with only three years of service. At one such meeting, some members complained about the cuts in the facilities provided for them. At first I tried to explain the position but they were not prepared to listen. After some time I lost my temper and told them that whatever I had done was in larger interests. I also said that under such circumstances, it was not possible for me to continue to remain at the mela site and that I would be leaving for the district headquarters. Some good elements in the committee reacted in my favour and tried to stop me from doing what I had proposed to do. But I was really angry and did not listen to anybody. I immediately went to my camp, where I dictated a wireless message for the collector and also booked a telephone call to him.

Fortunately, the call matured at once and the collector was also available. I explained the whole situation to him and sought his permission to leave the mela site. Firstly, he tried to console me saying that such happenings were the hazards of public administration. When I persisted in my resolution, he became tough and asked me not to leave the mela site. He said that if my objective was to fight against the negative elements, it would be defeated by my leaving the site and that was exactly what they wanted. In such a situation the positive elements would get disheartened and the purpose of the vested interests would be served. If at all anyone was to leave the mela site, it should be those elements who had complaints against the arrangements. The argument appeared very convincing to me. By that time, my agitation had died down and I accepted the advice of the collector. Fortunately, the wireless peon came back saying that the machine was not working and the message could not be passed through. Meanwhile the positive elements in the committee made my leaving the site an issue and prevailed upon the negative elements to make amends. They too came to me and pleaded for not leaving the site. Taking all these factors into consideration, I decided to stay back and thereafter there was no problem. The administration of the mela went on very smoothly. We were not only able to provide more facilities to the public but were also able to do so at a lesser cost. Incidentally the budget of the mela ended in a surplus against all previous records of deficit. Naturally it was appreciated by all and gave me a lot of satisfaction as well as confidence. In the process the negative elements also got demoralised. Of course, I was also cautious not to make them feel insulted and tried to take them into my confidence whenever necessary.

The morale of the incident is obvious. We all come across situations in life when we feel that positive elements are being harassed by negative elements. Quite often positive elements tend to quit and leave the field free for negative elements. This is what negative elements want. They know that they can never conquer the positive elements in a fair battle and want to win by default. Positive elements should understand this fact and not allow the battle to go by default. At times positive elements may not be prepared to fight but in that case they should make preparation and not give up the idea of fighting. Ultimately the triumph is always of the positive elements. In this battle the numbers are not very important. In the Mahabharata war five Pandavas were stronger than one hundred and one Kauravas. Here it is a question of moral strength which is missing in the negative elements. Normally, the negative elements flee once they find the positive elements ready to fight. Even if they are able to muster the support of other negative elements, they are internally weak. The battle should never be lost to them by giving them a walk-over.

This is what my collector meant when he asked me to stay back. His exact words were "Why should you quit?" I feel these are applicable to all positive elements in all situations. The only exception can be a tactical retreat. After all, at time, battles are lost to win a war and games are lost to win a match.

> Whenever you see a successful venture, it shows that someone made a courageous decision.

38
WHEN TEARS TURN THE LIFE

My spiritual master, Swami Bhoomanandji, comes to Delhi every year in the month of October/November. After public discourses for about two weeks, he pays house visits to his close devotees. Normally these visits exceed the originally planned number due to last minute requests. Devotees consider his visits a privilege and invite their friends and relatives to attend them. Swamiji undertakes such visits with great fondness and usually speaks on subjects which are highly relevant to day-to-day life. This generates a lot of interest and he receives requests for more visits. Of course, he tries to accept them to the extent possible.

During one such visit in 1992 held at a posh colony of New Delhi, I was also present with many others. Swamiji gave a short talk and thereafter invited devotees to ask questions. Among the devotees present, there was an elderly lady whose husband had died recently. The husband had been a diplomat and had held several important posts. He had lived a full life. It appeared that there had been a deep bond between the husband and the wife. Naturally, this death came as a great shock to her, which she was unable to bear. She was not able to accept the reality and sought Swamiji's guidance in the matter. She told Swamiji that she felt like weeping all the time and memories of her husband occupied her mind constantly.

Swamiji could understand the grief of the lady. He tried to console by telling her that death was a natural phenomenon, more so when one is in an advanced age. One of the spouses has to go first and in her case it happened to be the husband. He saw no cause for undue grief in such a natural happening. He did not go into the philosophical aspects of death and dealt with her problem in a humane manner. He also told her that if she felt like weeping, there was nothing wrong with it. After all, nature has provided us with tear glands for a purpose and we must make use of them whenever necessary. There should be no feeling of guilt in weeping. In fact, he advised her to weep regularly till she overcame her grief. However, he added that more important than weeping was her attitude and tears should help in making it positive. Fortunately, this had an impact on the lady and after about a week she invited Swamiji to her home. I happened to be there also and found the lady greatly changed.

This set me thinking about the role of tears in life, including my own. Normally, I am against weeping but I distinctly remember to have wept bitterly on a few occasions in my life and every time I emerged a stronger person. In fact, such occasions turned the course of my life and, needless to say, it was for the better.

Here, I would like to classify weeping into two kinds. One is negative weeping and the other positive. If the process of weeping leads to depression, fear and frustration, I would call it negative weeping. It changes life for the worse. On the other hand, if the process of weeping leads to introspection, courage and determination, it can be called positive weeping. It turns the life for the better. Thus tears are the turning points in life. It is up to us how we use them for our elevation or depression.

Coming to the attitude towards weeping, it can be said that a wise person, having understood the fundamentals of life will see no occasion to weep. For him good or bad events of life are alike. However, this kind of attitude is not expected from ordinary mortals. For them there is a clear distinction between good and bad events. It is for them that weeping helps. In fact, it is healthier to weep than to camouflage grief. Weeping helps in overcoming grief and if such a person gets the company of the wise, tears turn the life for the better. This is what happened to the lady who came in contact with Swamiji in New Delhi.

Tears are the detergent of soul.

39
PEACE AT ANY PRICE IS CHEAP

I had a cousin who passed away in April 1991 at the age of 58 when he underwent a second bypass surgery in U.K. We were very close to each other with deep mutual respect. Though he was older than me, we used to have very meaningful discussions. He also acted as my guide during the initial years of my career. When I passed my engineering examination from the University of Roorkee, he advised me to join private sector. I followed his advice but subsequently providence brought me into the IAS and he was one of the happiest persons on this development. In the later years, he changed his opinion about government service and wanted his son to join the IAS. However, he joined IIM Calcutta, and is today very well settled.

The reason why he changed his opinion was perhaps his adoption of an integrated view of life. He himself had had a brilliant career as a chartered accountant and served in some very good private companies where he worked with great dedication. Unfortunately he developed a coronary problem and underwent a bypass surgery in U.K. Thereafter he continued to live cheerfully for years until he was advised to undergo another operation. He decided to get operated at the same place and by the same surgeon who had operated him earlier. He left India for his second surgery on 8 April, 1991. On that day I spent about an hour with him in the morning. When I was taking leave of him, he gave me a word of advice saying, "Rakesh, remember one thing — Peace at any price is cheap." Obviously it was the essence of his life which I took with great reverence and emotion.

This was our last meeting. After a week or so, we got the news of his passing away. The will of God was to be accepted but his last message still keeps ringing in my ears. The more I contemplate over the message, the more I find it true and relevant. Only about a year before his passing away, I had founded a mission called 'Kabir Peace Mission'. In the preamble of its aims and objects, the word 'Peace' was defined as 'Integrated Development'. I am of the view that any development should lead to peace and if it does not happen, it is not real development. Similarly, when we think of progress or development in life, peace should be its natural corollary. If it is not so, there is something wrong in the so-called progress or development.

Today peace eludes most of us despite all our achievements. I know several friends and relatives who have everything to make an impressive biodata but do not have peace of mind. The question arises — what is it that goes wrong? The intention here is not to discuss the subject from a very philosophical point of view but to establish the fact that even from the materialistic point of view, it is necessary to understand certain facts of life. There is no doubt that we all need material progress. The error most of us commit is that we make this progress the end and not the means. I look at material progress only as a means to achieve the ultimate aim, which is peace of mind. Very few are able to discriminate between the two and no wonder that peace eludes most of us.

In the name of progress, we forget our essential needs. We do not know the amount of money we need, the size of the house we require, and the number of clothes we should own. Most of our time and energy are wasted in increasing them rather than using or enjoying what we already possess. The result is that while we may be in a position to afford very good food, we have no time or appetite to enjoy it. We may be having a big house with lawns, but have no time or mood to relax. We may have a large number of friends and relatives but have no time to spend with them.

My cousin had seen life closely and God had given him the wisdom to understand it fully. In giving his advice on the choice of career, his intention was not to compare jobs but to emphasise the fact that life was to be seen as a package. Any package which offers greater peace of mind was to be preferred over the others. Perhaps, he realised that a government job was a better package because of its stability and well defined limits. As far as his own career was concerned, he was highly respected in all the organisations where he had worked and his physical problem was not necessarily due to pressures of job. Irrespective of all these, the message given by him is an important fact of life. Those who understand and absorb it, can hope to lead a happy life. Peace will come to them without paying any price.

- A great part of the happiness of life consists not in fighting battles, but in avoiding them.
- A masterly retreat is in itself a victory.
- A peace that depends on fear is a suppressed war.
- Flying from work is never the way to find peace.
- Peace hath her victories. No less renown'd than war.
- Peace is a condition of the mind, the undisturbed state of mind.

40

BE DANGEROUSLY HONEST

In April 1994, when I was living in R.K.Puram at New Delhi, an elderly friend of mine came to stay with us for a few days. I consider him to be like my elder brother. During his stay, he desired to visit Shri Dharam Veera, an ex-ICS officer who had occupied many important positions including the governorship of West Bengal and Karnataka. They hailed from the same village. In all his assignments, Dharam Veera had done remarkably well. A man of courage and integrity, he never compromised in matters of principles. In our student days, we used to hold him in high esteem. So when my friend expressed a desire to visit Dharam Veera, I also became interested and we both went to see him one evening.

We found him quite active even at his advanced age. He kept himself involved in many important activities. It was a matter of privilege to spend some time with him. He narrated several interesting events of his life, which gave me a lot of inspiration. Perhaps, he also developed some liking for me during our brief meeting. When our discussion was coming to an end, I asked him for a message for those who want to work with honesty and sincerity. He very happily gave me two points of advice. First of all he said, an honest person should be fearless. Not only this, he should instil fear in the wicked and confidence among the good. He used the words 'Dangerously honest' while explaining what he meant. His second piece of advice was that an administrator should be as helpful as possible. He advised for positive interpretation of the rules so long as no self-interest was involved. According to him serving people is a rare opportunity and one should not lose it by looking too much into rules and regulations. I took his advice seriously and contemplated over it. I am going to share here my contemplation over the first advice.

I feel pained when people say that honesty does not pay in the present circumstances. This feeling prevails not only among civil servants but among all classes. What is more painful is that such a feeling exists even among some of already handful honest people. These so-called honest people display this feeling when they present a gloomy picture of their lives before others. This damages the system all the more. I feel that such people are either not honest in the true sense or are ignorant of the full dimensions of honesty. A person with an integrated view of honesty has no occasion to complain. For him honesty remains a source of strength and he finds no clash between his ways and the working of the system. I will give here two examples to explain what I am trying to say.

I met a businessman on board a plane while travelling from Calcutta to Delhi. He appeared to be a very simple man. He was carrying a cloth bag containing tea packets. He was a big businessman with an income running into crores. He owned tea-gardens and several other businesses. He told me that about 50 years back, he started his career on a meagre salary of rupees eight per month. When asked the secret of his success, unhesitatingly he told me that it was on account of his honest hard work.

The second interaction was on Rajdhani Express when I was travelling from Calcutta to Kanpur. There I met a senior advocate of Allahabad. He had been in the legal profession for about 40 years and was one of the leading lawyers of the town. When asked whether it was possible for an honest and sincere law graduate to set up a good legal practice, he replied in the affirmative. He added that honesty and sincerity were the secrets of his success.

While it may be too simplistic to establish the strength of honesty on the basis of these two examples, they do establish my point to a great extent. There is no doubt that there are many aberrations in the system but to say that they can be taken care of by dishonest means is not at all correct. Such an approach only adds to the aberrations and least wonder that today we find ourselves in a situation which appears to be hopeless. If corrections are to be made, it is possible only through honest means. What is, perhaps, required in addition to honesty, is practical wisdom. The problem with many honest persons is that for them honesty becomes an end and not the means. After all, one has to be honest for some purpose and if the purpose is not achieved, the honesty becomes meaningless. At times an honest person may become a victim of the system but to condemn honesty on this ground is not at all justified. If we go by this criterion, surely the chances of falling victims are much more on the path of dishonesty. If we take an integrated view of life, I am sure the path of honesty will turn out to be more rewarding than the path of dishonesty.

This is perhaps what persons like Dharam Veera, the businessman I met on the plane, and the advocate I came across on the train had in mind when they advocated the path of honesty in the closing years of their lives. It is not that these persons had seen only success in life. Surely there must have been ups and downs but they grew steadily with them and refused to bow down in adverse situations. Perhaps, it is not possible for a dishonest person to understand the strength of honesty. I do not think a truly honest person has any regret in following the path of honesty. It is only those who do not take an integrated view of honesty, that find themselves in pitiable conditions despite being honest. The need is to understand the difference between being honest for the sake of honesty and being honest for the sake of a cause. In the first case, honesty becomes the end while in the latter it is the means. Those who are honest for a cause gain strength and have no complaints. Not only this, they are considered to be dangerous by the dishonest. The advice of becoming 'dangerously honest' is thus literally true.

41

THE WEALTH OF NATURE

I remained posted at Kanpur for full six years. This period marked a turning point in my life from many points of view. In this period I developed close relations with many people which led to the formation of the 'Kabir Peace Mission'. Most of these contacts began in my official capacity but turned into personal relations. Some of them are now closer to me than my blood relations. One such relation is a nephew of mine who used to play tennis with me regularly. Naturally, he became very close to me. Apart from playing tennis, we used to exchange views on many subjects. As a result we developed a mutual liking.

This boy subsequently shifted to Mumbai for business. His father bought a flat for him in the posh area of Cuffe Parade costing over a crore of rupees. The flat is not very big and has only two bedrooms. I was very happy with this development and was keen to visit him in Mumbai at the earliest opportunity. And this opportunity came in March 1993 when I visited Mumbai on my way to Kudremukh. At Bombay I stayed in a guest house which was located in a building adjacent to the one in which my nephew lived. In the evening I went to his flat. He very fondly took me to every corner of his flat and described its positive features. What amused me most was his statement that apart from other features, the good thing about the flat was that it had sunlight and also air. I lightly commented that if even after paying over a crore rupees, the flat would not have air and light then of what worth would it be to? Then he explained me that air and light were luxuries in a city like Mumbai and he was lucky to have such a flat. He also gave many examples where fresh air was not available even after paying larger amounts. The matter ended there.

I got another opportunity to visit Mumbai after a year or so. That time I stayed in our own guest house which was located in Bandra. I reached there late in the evening. Mumbai remains quite warm even in the month of November and the use of air-conditioners is quite common. Since I was tired I also slept with the air-conditioner on and woke up a little later than my usual time. When I opened the windows of my room, I saw a cluster of multi-storeyed buildings all around. Then I closely looked at the building opposite to ours. The sun had risen and for many it was the office-going time. What I saw was once again amusing. In some of the flats of the opposite building, the residents had tied ropes for drying washed clothes. Since the rope was outside the window, they were using special devices for putting clothes over the rope and the same exercise was being done for removing the dried clothes.

When I talked about it with my local officer over breakfast, he told me that the residents of that building were lucky to have sunlight at least on the outer walls of their flats. In his flat sunlight was not available at all. As a result the clothes had to be dried inside the rooms.

This set me thinking about the bounties which nature provides us in abundance. For most of us, things like air and sun go unnoticed and we take them for granted. We affix no value to them unless we live in places as mentioned above. Our whole value system is based on material acquisitions only and it is no wonder that we deprive ourselves of the wealth, nature has given us. In the process we also lose the pleasure of our material wealth to a great extent. In fact, a balance between these two aspects of wealth must be struck for a truly enjoyable life. So we should equally respect the wealth of nature and those who do not have much of the material wealth should not feel unduly poor. In all probability they enjoy a bigger share of nature's wealth, though they may not be attributing any price to it. Even if we look into the subject purely from the economic point of view, it can be established that what nature provides is priceless. For survival, the gifts of nature are more essential than the creation of human beings. In fact, all wealth originates from nature including the wealth created by man. Looking from this point of view a poor man is wealthier, since he enjoys a bigger share of the priceless wealth of nature.

Be Thankful

Be thankful, that you don't have everything you desire.
If you did, what would there be to look forward to ?
Be thankful, when you don't know something.
For it gives you the opportunity to learn.
Be thankful, for the difficult times.
It is during those times that you grow.
Be thankful, for your limitations,
Because they give you opportunities for improvement.
Be thankful, for each new challenge,
For that will build your strength and character.
Be thankful, for your mistakes.
They will teach you valuable lessons.
Be thankful, when you're tired and weary,
Because it means you've made an effort.
It's easy to be thankful for the good things in life.
But a life of rich fulfillment comes to those,
Who are also thankful for their setbacks.

42

LIVING PERFECTLY

My wife is a very good lady but the world around her keeps upsetting her every now and then. However, the frequency is going down with the growth of wisdom. Once, she got upset over a matter, which was quite justified for a normal person but not for a truly wise one. While I took worldly care of her grievance, I was unhappy over her lack of wisdom in dealing with the situation. So sometime after the event, I sat with her and helped in her introspection. Fortunately she was responsive and I could convince her that there was no point in getting upset due to the imperfections of the world as it would continue to remain so. The only solution was to learn living perfectly in an imperfect world. Thereafter, I did some contemplation over the subject and this is what I am sharing here.

    First of all I admit that it is not as simple as said. The imperfections of the world do upset us and we have all the justification to complain. Some complaints may even be helpful but surely one cannot make the world perfect. In fact, imperfection is necessary for the existence of the world. Even the creation of the world was the result of an imperfection. The word creation implies dynamism and there can be no dynamism without imbalance of forces which in turn means imperfection. In a state of perfection nothing will move and perhaps the world itself will cease to exist. So for the existence of the world, imperfection is necessary.

    The purpose of this analysis is to make one accept the imperfectness of the world as a reality. This acceptance will itself help us not to get upset most of the time but surely the end objective is not achieved. This stage in essence implies tolerance of the world which is not a perfectly healthy stage. It points towards hidden anger which is an obstruction in one's growth. A person with such an attitude will perhaps not be able to lessen the imperfections of the world. At best he will not add to them. There is also a possibility of his crossing the threshold limit in a more upsetting situation and thus taking him to the state of reaction from tolerance.

Now arises the question how to rise above the state of 'tolerance' which I would call the state of 'acceptance'. Here the word 'acceptance' is not being used as something passive. In fact, it indicates a state of extreme dynamism which means appearing static due to fast motion. To reach this state, one has to see that imperfectness of the world as an opportunity to make oneself perfect. So when you see a poor person, a feeling of sharing should develop. A person in distress should evoke compassion in you. An angry person should create a feeling of love. A person trying to harm you should be seen as ignorant. Outwardly we may behave in a worldly manner depending upon the situation, but within, the feeling should always be one of dynamic acceptance. If one is able to reach this state, he will never complain about the imperfectness of the world. On the other hand, he will silently contribute to lessen this imperfectness by making himself perfect. After all, the world is constituted of individuals and the imperfectness of the world is nothing but the sum-total of the imperfectness of individuals. So making oneself perfect automatically lessens the imperfectness of the world.

Next time you come across an imperfect situation, see it as an opportunity, for making yourself perfect. In this process your attitude towards those who upset you will change. You will then feel that such persons are like a ladder which helps you to rise above and to make you perfect. And living perfectly is the only option in this imperfect world.

> Aim at perfection in everything, but don't lose sight of the objective for its sake.

43

WHEN YOU GROW WISE

In November 1993, I was appointed as a central observer of the Election Commission for the Himachal Pradesh Assembly Elections. Just before leaving for my first visit to the state, I developed a severe pain in my wisdom tooth. I consulted a senior dentist who advised immediate extraction of the tooth and called me the next day. I was not prepared for this because I didn't want to lose the tooth so early. Though I had crossed 44, my teeth had been in a good condition. So I consulted another dentist friend who advised me to wait for some time more as the pain could be managed with the help of medicines. Somehow the election duty was carried out without much difficulty.

The problem became acute once again in November 1994 at Calcutta. This time again, the dentist advised extraction of the wisdom tooth. He told me that there was no function of wisdom teeth after a certain age and that I need not be unduly concerned about losing one of them. I found his explanation convincing. Next day he removed the tooth and I got relief.

Somehow the word 'wisdom' got registered in my mind and I discussed it with my medical consultant. I wanted to know the reason for these teeth being called wisdom teeth. Though he couldn't give me a satisfactory explanation, he told me that these teeth grow after crossing the teens, i.e., in the early twenties and generally have to be removed in the forties. This information was enough for me to contemplate over the matter and I arrived at certain conclusions which I am going to share here.

Human life has always been divided into four phases. In our scriptures these phases are called *Brahmacharya, Grastha, Van Prastha* and *Sanyasa*, respectively. Assuming an ideal lifespan of 100 years each phase comes to about 25 years. However, in real life, a good lifespan may be taken as about 80 years. So each phase of life is of about 20 years.

The first phase of life, *Brahmacharya*, is a phase of restraint and learning. Those who wish to acquire anything in life have to remain disciplined and work hard during this period. The full meaning of life is hardly understood in this period. In a way it is good also. If life is understood in totality during this period, perhaps the urge to learn and acquire knowledge would be lost. Acquisition of mundane knowledge during this period is essential to successfully live the subsequent phases of life. This phase is like the running of an aeroplane on the ground before take-off. If sufficient speed is not acquired on the runway, the plane cannot take off and at times may meet with an accident.

The second phase of life is the most difficult one and can be compared to the take-off of an aeroplane. During this phase, one has to rise above the ground and achieve worldly success. Maximum energy is consumed during this period and the knowledge acquired during the first phase of life is to be applied. One comes across a variety of experiences and we gain maturity and wisdom as a result of these interactions. While in the first phase of our life, one only acquires knowledge and remains on ground, in the second phase one acquires wisdom and gains height. That is why the wisdom teeth grow only in the early twenties. Their appearance thus indicates that the time for acquiring wisdom has come.

The acquisition of wisdom has also to come to an end. A period of 20-25 years in the second phase of life should be sufficient for a person to understand life fully and to acquire wisdom. It is like acquiring full height by an aeroplane during a flight. After acquiring this height, there is no need of going higher and the acquired height should be enjoyed. In human life this stage should reach at the age of 40-45 years and one should be able to grow fully wise by this time. At this stage, there is no need of wisdom teeth and that is why they are no more required. I feel that this could be the reason behind these teeth being called wisdom teeth.

Having grown wise, one enters the third phase of life. For a truly wise person, life should become smooth in this phase and he should be able to enjoy it like an aeroplane journey in the third stage. There is no need of any imposed restrictions in this phase and the gains of life are to be shared. A wise person should share his acquisitions including wisdom for his inner expansion as the outer expansion is no more required. If one does not share, in all probability he is heading for a miserable fourth phase of life.

The fourth phase of life is like the landing of an aeroplane. In this phase the acquired height is to be lost in order to land safely. If it is not done, a crash is inevitable. What does it mean in terms of life? It means that a time comes in life when even wisdom has to be transcended. After all, in this cycle of birth and death, there are others in the queue and one should voluntarily make way for them. If one does not do so, he will either be pushed or crushed. A truly wise person should avoid this situation. That is why this phase of life is called Sanyasa ashram. One has to give up everything for a happy end.

Thus the four phases of life are the phases of acquiring knowledge, acquiring wisdom, sharing wisdom and transcending wisdom. The extraction of wisdom tooth indicates that the period of acquiring wisdom is over. It is like taking away the answer book by the invigilator at the end of the prescribed time, no matter whether one has completed it or not. So you should grow wise before your wisdom tooth is extracted.

> True wisdom is freedom from self-esteem, hypocrisy and injury to others.

44
COUNTDOWN FOR LAUNCHING

In my early childhood, I lived with my elder sister for some time. She had been then recently married and her husband was posted in a small town of Gorakhpur District in U.P. There a tutor was arranged for me. He was quite elderly and was known as Maulvi Sahab. Though not very soothing by looks, he was very affectionate and concerned about my studies. However, I did not feel very comfortable in his company. One of the pet exercises he used to give me was to do reverse counting. Somehow I did not like it as I could never understand its logic. However, in due course his sincerity won me and we developed a congenial relationship.

The same exercise of reverse counting was subsequently given to my son by a famous ayurvedic doctor of Calcutta. I had taken my son to him because of his lack of concentration in his studies. When asked, the doctor told me that reverse counting was one of the methods of developing concentration. I saw logic in it and naturally my memory took me to my childhood, reminding me of the exercise given by the Maulvi Sahab. It also reminded me of our visit to ISRO, Trivandrum many years ago. There we saw the launching of a rocket and carefully noted the countdown before it took off. Somehow the word 'Countdown' stuck in my mind and I thought over it philosophically. This is what I am going to share in this write-up.

First of all we must understand that a rocket is a device which is used for sending a satellite or any other object in the space. For this purpose it should be able to provide enough power so as to impart escape velocity to the object. Once this object achieves escape velocity, it reaches the space provided the direction of the launching is correct. Thus we need to have two factors, namely, power and direction for putting an object into a space orbit. When the object reaches the right orbit, no more power is required and it remains in motion due to gravitational forces. As the object goes higher and higher, the fuel chambers of the rocket are released one by one till the object is put into the orbit when no more fuel is required.

Let us compare this situation with the process of self-realisation. Here the objective is the merger of our little self with the cosmic power which may be called 'God'. For this also a similar strategy has to be adopted. The 'self' here would be the object to be launched in the space and the mind would be the rocket. The first step in the launching of the rocket is the countdown. What does it mean in the case of mind? It means that it has to be emptied from worldly thoughts, if we want it to rise above the world. That is to say, it has to reach the stage of 'zero' before taking off. For most of us the problem lies here. We fill up our minds with so many worldly thoughts that it is not able to rise above the world permanently. Occasionally we may develop detachment but the attractions of the world pull us back. Only a fortunate few are able to reach the stage of 'zero' which is necessary for the take-off. It is like committing mistakes in reverse counting and very few reach the zero level without making any errors. Somewhere or the other we get strangled.

Having reached the stage of 'zero', the mind has to develop enough power to impart 'escape velocity' to the 'self'. If this is not done, it will never be able to rise above the body which may be compared to the earth in the case of a satellite. Not only this, the direction of the motion should also be correct. That is why the power of the mind, when applied in the wrong direction, not only fails to achieve the objective but also does great harm. For this, one may also seek the help of a spiritual master, whose instructions may not be liked in the beginning but his sincerity is bound to prevail, if the seeker is serious. Once the process of self-realisation is complete, it hardly needs any effort to stay there. The only requirement is that the components of the object/satellite should function well and they should be maintained properly. In case of a self-realised person it may be said that his body and mind should function well and they should be given due care. Of course, nothing can be done beyond natural limitations.

Thus we find that 'countdown' is the first necessary step for launching. This is true of all spheres of life, be they spiritual or mundane. Even for worldly achievements, one has to empty oneself of other thoughts and impart full energy in the correct direction. That is why the famous philosopher, J. Krishnamurti, used to say: 'Unlearning is the beginning of learning'. We may also say that "Countdown is the beginning of Launching".

> He who has not turned away from evil conduct, whose senses are uncontrolled, who is not tranquil, whose mind is not at rest, he can never attain this Great Self even by knowledge.
> — Katha - Upanishad

45
GANGA OR SAGAR ?

India is a country of holy places. Most people consider it a privilege to go on pilgrimage to these places. It is a great pleasure to see people undertaking all sorts of troubles in order to visit these places, which are not always comfortable. In this respect they show tremendous faith and patience. I have great reverence for this aspect of our culture and consider it a source of strength of our nation. It is a different matter that the objective of undertaking a pilgrimage is not always the same that it should be.

I have had the privilege of visiting many holy places belonging to different religions. While I have no craving for these places, I like to visit them. In fact, more than the places, I enjoy the pilgrims and their faith. Here I am going to share some of the thoughts which came to my mind during our recent visit to Ganga Sagar.

Ganga Sagar is one of the most revered places of the Hindus. This is located in West Bengal and here the river Ganges merges into the ocean. It is said that while other holy places should be visited several times, it is enough to visit the Ganga Sagar only once. This belief may be due to the difficult journey for the Ganga Sagar in the past. Now, of course, it is not so and the journey can be undertaken easily. But somehow the same belief continues.

After being posted to Calcutta, in July 1994, it had been our wish also to visit the Ganga Sagar and the opportunity came in

December 1994. In November 1994, I got a letter from my former director of National Academy of Administration, Shri Rajeshwar Prasad, expressing his wish to visit the Ganga Sagar and enquiring whether it would be possible to arrange the same. I was very happy to receive this letter for two reasons. Firstly, it gave me an opportunity to plan our visit also and, secondly, undertaking this pilgrimage with him was to be an added pleasure. So everything was planned in detail and we undertook this pilgrimage towards the end of December. The district collector was of great help in making local arrangements and there was no difficulty of any kind.

During our stay at the Ganga Sagar, we had a good bath. While taking bath a thought came to my mind whether we were taking bath in Ganga or Sagar. The merger was so complete that it was difficult to differentiate one from the other. Some said it was Ganga and others felt it was Sagar. This made me think of the difference between the two. After all, Mother Ganga was a creation of the ocean only. Even when we see this holy river as a separate entity, is it not part of the same Creator, that is, the ocean? In our ignorance we see them as separate entities. The ultimate aim of Mother Ganga is the merger with its creator and that is what happens at Ganga Sagar. It is like the merger of 'Jiva' with the 'Brahma'. Due to ignorance, we consider 'Jiva' as a separate entity from 'Brahma' while they are actually the same. Somehow the course of nature keeps drawing 'Jiva' towards 'Brahma' till they merge in the end. The ultimate aim of life is this merger and having attained it, there is nothing else to aim for.

This is what happens at Ganga Sagar also. Here the Mother Ganga, a creation of the ocean, merges with the Creator and thereafter it has to go nowhere. The cycle of creation and merger completes here and the process continues. The same is true of our life cycle also. The created keeps merging into the Creator and the cycle continues. This also explains the belief that while other holy places should be visited several times, it is enough to visit the Ganga Sagar only once. After all, having attained the supreme goal, what remains to be attained ? Only a fortunate few reach this goal and it is no wonder that those who are able to undertake the pilgrimage to Ganga Sagar are considered fortunate.

- What we experience in the depths of our souls is realisation.
- When a man realises, he gives up everything.

46

LIFE IS A PROCESS OF WEEDING

Weeding is an important aspect of office working. There are rules and regulations on the subject and every office is supposed to follow them. The purpose is to weed our unnecessary/obsolete papers at definite intervals so that the office remains tidy and works with greater efficiency. I take special interest in this area. During my inspection of any office I pay great attention towards cleanliness and check whether timely weeding has been carried out or not. I am of the view that those who pay attention to this aspect of office working, are also efficient in other areas. In fact, whenever I join a new office, I personally carry out this exercise in my own office. This not only helps me in my working but also motivates my colleagues to do the same.

Weeding is equally important in plant life. In order to get a healthy crop, one has to ensure that weeds are removed in time. I remember when I was posted as district collector, the agricultural secretary at that time had launched a special weeding drive for the wheat crop. That year the problem of a particular weed in the crop of wheat had been very acute. The secretary's motivated call for the weeding programme drew a healthy response from all concerned. As a result, the average yield of wheat in the state went up substantially and the Central Government gave a special award to the state for this achievement.

Extending the above logic further, I want to establish that weeding is equally important for a healthy human life. We all know that life is a process of change and if one does not outgrow the past continuously, one will neither be able to enjoy the present nor think of the future. I had an occasion to think about this subject once when I was preparing my new year's diary. I am going to share my thoughts in this write-up.

While making notes from the previous year's diary, I came across several references and addresses which appeared to be very relevant and close at the time of writing but were now totally irrelevant. For a moment there was a temptation to note them also. Previously I had a tendency to be overcautious and used to note down everything in the hope of their distant utility. However, such an eventuality was rare and such notes only proved to be a burden on the mind. That year I decided that if a reference or address had not been used for the past 2 to 3 years, there was no point in carrying it over any longer. As a result of this criterion, many references and addresses were weeded out and my new year's diary became much more manageable. Not only this, the load on the mental span decreased and the focus on the present and the future improved.

Some philosophical thoughts also came to mind in this process. For a moment I thought whether weeding is a positive phenomenon or a negative one. My contemplation established that it is a positive phenomenon from every point of view. Even in worldly life we find that life is a process of quitting and getting. When one gets a promotion, one quits the lower post. When a student is promoted to a higher class, he quits the lower one. When one constructs a house in a bigger town, one quits the smaller one. When one buys a car, one quits the lower mode of transport. There may be innumerable examples of such kind. Do we call such quitting a negative action ? No, by all means they are positive actions provided the ego is not there. Here I am talking of a natural phenomenon happening in one's life. Therefore, we must use the word 'transcending' in place of 'quitting'. From this point of view every process of weeding is a transcending process.

Looking from another point of view, it is also a fact that if we don't leave things, things will leave us. In that case the process may be painful. After all, in this transitory world, how can we expect things to remain with us forever ? If so, the wisdom lies in

Life Is A Process Of Weeding

quitting them before they quit us. If we do so, we save ourselves from the agony of separation. Not only this, we are left with more energy for rising higher and higher.

Thus we find that constant weeding is essential for moving on to a higher path in life. It is true in the field of materials, in the field of plants and equally in the field of human life. Those who understand and follow this, enjoy a healthy and purposeful life. For such people, the whole life becomes a process of weeding and they do not get perturbed when the time for the weeding of the body itself arrives.

> We do not count a man's years,
> until he has nothing else to count.
> Age is a quality of mind.
> If you have left your dreams behind,
> If you no longer look ahead,
> If your ambition's fires are dead .....
> Then you are old !
> But if from life you take the best,
> And if in life you keep the zest,
> If love you hold,
> No matter how the years go by,
> No matter how the birthdays fly ....
> You are not old !
>
> — *Ralph Waldo Emerson*

47

I HAVE NO ENEMY

The incident relates to the year 1984. In the month of January, I had gone to Varanasi where I visited the DIG of Police in his home. There I met an elderly person, Mr. Kejriwal, who had good business at Varanasi and Bombay. His son was settled in Varanasi while he himself lived in Bombay. During our brief meeting, we developed a liking for each other. Incidentally, I was to visit Bombay in the following month only. He invited me to visit his place and I promised to do so.

 I spent about an hour with him in Bombay at his residence. His flat was quite big and was located on the main Marine Drive. I had not been much exposed to Bombay at that time, so I was quite impressed. However, his lifestyle appeared to be quite simple. During our talks, I asked him about his friends. To this he gave a very unusual reply. He said that he didn't know the number of his friends but definitely he had no enemy. Though impressed by this reply, I was not able to understand the depth of his answer. Subsequently I contemplated over this reply of his for a long time and understood its depth. This is what I am going to share in this write-up.

 First of all I am of the view that friendship as well as enmity are only the states of mind. There are different qualities of them which depend upon the growth of mind. Generally the quality of friendship or enmity is determined by the motive we have in mind. The lower motive leads to lower quality of friendship and vice versa. There are different degrees of this quality. As we grow internally and expand our vision, the feeling of enmity starts disappearing and a time comes when one reaches the state Mr Kejriwal had attained. An ordinary mortal may not find it easy to reach this state but there can be no doubt that all of us should strive to reach this state. A scientific analysis of the subject will be helpful to expedite the process.

At this point an incident of Shri Ishwarchandra Vidyasagar's life comes to my mind. He was a very learned person and at the same time very humble. He always tried to be helpful to others. Most of us must have read about the incident when he worked as a coolie for someone who considered it below his dignity to carry a small suitcase at a railway station. Once a well-wisher of him brought to his notice an adverse comment made by someone about him. Shri Vidyasagar responded in a very strange manner. He said that he was unable to understand the cause of the adverse comment because he had never helped that person. The message was that only those whom we help criticise us and it is up to us how we respond to that criticism.

A person with a lower mind will immediately develop a feeling of enmity towards such a person and the friendship will turn into enmity. Naturally such friendship is of a lower kind where the motives are selfish. In order to avoid such situations, one has to rise higher and develop a friendship without any motive. Nothing should be expected in return. Only such a friendship can stand the test of time. It is not that there is no worldly return from such a friendship. In fact, from the worldly point of view also such a friendship is very rewarding. The only difference is that a selfless friendship always gives joy and the situation of pain does never arise.

Well, if this becomes the criterion of our friendship where is the question of enmity ? Thus we can say that only a lower kind of friendship or relationship changes into enmity. Numerous examples can be given to establish that most of the enemies were good friends at one time. It was only the lower nature of their friendship that turned them into enemies. Therefore, the best way to avoid such a situation is to develop only a higher kind of friendship where the motive is only to offer and not to receive. Having reached this stage, one not only enjoys the joy of friendship, one also gets rid of the pain of the enmity. A single thought of enmity may give us more pain than many thoughts of friendship. From this point of view also it becomes more important to have no enemy than to have many friends. Therefore, a 'no enemy situation' automatically means a state of universal friendship.

Friendship being a state of mind has no physical connotation. Others may consider you as their enemy but you will not do so. In such a state of mind, even killing becomes a friendly act. We all know that when Lord Rama killed Ravana, he had no feeling of enmity towards him. This was proved by the reverence shown by Him towards Ravana during his last moments. Our target should be to reach this 'No Enemy' state in order to enjoy life. Perhaps Mr Kejriwal had reached it when he said "I have no enemy".

- Be slow to give your friendship, but when you have given it strive to make it lasting.
- Counsel of good friends is useful when your own self-love impairs your judgement.
- Friends are made by many acts, but are lost by one act.
- It is chance that makes brothers but hearts that make friends.
- Success depends on your ability to make and keep friends.
- The ornament of a house is the friends who frequent it.

48
LEADING A SIMPLE LIFE

"Simple living and high thinking" is a common phrase to describe many great persons of this country. In my childhood this phrase was commonly used for personalities like Dr Rajendra Prasad, Pandit Jawaharlal Nehru, Pandit Govind Ballabh Pant and many other living at that time. Shri Lal Bahadur Shastri fitted the description aptly and was greatly revered for his simple living. All these people occupied high positions at one time or another. Naturally, they had all the perks and facilities attached to those high positions. And all such perks do not necessarily fall in the category of simplicity, seen from a common sense of the term.

One day in Kanpur in November 1994, I was sitting at the dining table in the company of good friends. The talk began with a discussion on simple food and we were trying to define it. Gradually the discussion shifted to the definition of a 'simple life'. The point of discussion was whether simple life implied deprivation or renunciation of material comforts which one gets in natural course. From this point of view many of the great men known for their simplicity did not lead a simple life. There are many persons who travel all the time by air, stay in comfortable places and eat costly food. Nevertheless it could be unfair to keep them out from the category of simple people on this ground. At the same time, there are many who do not get any of these facilities but still do not fall in the category of simple persons. All this led us to the conclusion that simplicity is something internal and not external. A person looking simple externally may not be so while a person appearing very comfortable may be quite simple within. Thus simplicity is in one way a state of mind.

To elaborate it further, it may be said that an effortless living falls in the category of simplicity. A person who neither rejoices over comforts nor mourns the lack of them is a simple person in true sense. Such a person does not hesitate to give up any article of comfort, when required to do so. Nor does he hanker after such objects, when he is not in a position to have them. If at all he uses certain facilities provided to him by virtue of his position and status, he does so with a detached state of mind. To an ordinary person he may appear to be living in luxury but is in fact above them. He looks upon them as something which helps him to discharge his duties efficiently.

In other words, a simple person is the same within and without. He does not boast about his surroundings nor does he hide anything. His life is very transparent. However, at times he has to use his discretion to decide whether certain facilities are actually required for discharging his duties or they have been added simply to raise his status. If so, such facilities should be done away with before he gets used to them. This is what is missing today. The holders of high office have made their environment luxurious from comfortable. While comfort may be desirable, luxury is certainly not. At times the line between the two is thin and at this point the holder of the office has to use his discrimination with firmness. This not only keeps the sycophants away, it infuses greater confidence and regard in the common people.

Many great people whom we know for their simplicity fell in this category. Unfortunately the number of such people is coming down. Even some of very rich persons like G D Birla and J R D Tata fall in the category of simple people. They accumulated no wealth for themselves. They worked for a higher pursuit and creation of wealth was just a natural process for them and they used it for the service of the nation at large. We need many more such persons today in every walk of life.

Simplicity has its own rewards. It gives tremendous inner strength to its possessor. A simple person is free from all kinds of fear, leading to a contented, healthy and meaningful life. He has nothing to boast about and nothing to hide. He is free from conflicts and achieves his goal effortlessly. Simplicity coupled with wisdom is a great strength. Thus from every point of view simplicity is a desirable quality. Let us all try to lead a simple life.

How poor we are !

One day a rich father took his son on a trip to the countryside, with the firm purpose to show him how poor people can be.

They spent a day and a night in the farm of a very poor family. When they got back from their trip the father asked his son, "How do you think was the trip, my son ?"

"Very good Dad !" replied the son.

"Did you see, how poor people can be ?"

"Yeah !"

"And what did you learn ?" the father asked.

The son answered, "I saw that we have one dog at home, and they have four. We have a pool that is hundred meters long, they have a stream that has no end. We have fifty imported lamps in our garden, they have countless shining stars. Our terrace reaches to the front yard, they have a whole horizon."

When the little boy was finishing, his father was speechless.

His son concluded, "Thanks Dad, for showing me how poor we are !"

49

WHEN YOU MISS YOUR WISH

In December 1994, I stayed at the Tata Steel Plant at Jamshedpur in connection with a joint plant committee meeting. The two days' stay was very well organised by TISCO. Apart from the meeting, visits to the plant, township, social activity centres, etc., were also arranged. In fact, the social welfare aspect of the Tatas is worth seeing and gives an indication of the philosophy as well as the vision of the founder Tatas. At Jamshedpur, a museum named "Russi Modi Centre of Excellence" has been recently established. It gives a complete picture of the history of the Tatas. I liked this place most and it left a deep mark on my mind. At this centre, I came across a biographical work on J R D Tata and subsequently a copy of the book was presented to me.

We all generally know about the great men and women of the nation and the world. However, going through their autobiographies and biographies one understands the real depth of their personalities. Somehow I like going through such works. I keenly glanced through the book on that day and subsequently read it closely. Naturally I learnt many things about the Tatas which were not known to me earlier. One such fact is that JRD had no child of his own. Despite this he had developed such a broad vision that this loss was hardly reflected anywhere. Occasionally in private conversation, he used to refer to this aspect of his life. But in no way did it constrain his vision or thinking. On the other hand, he treated all his employees as his family members and never considered his huge empire as a personal possession. As a matter of policy the Tatas provided suitable employment for at least one of the wards of their employees. This act developed so much feeling of belonging in the employees that they put their head and heart for the organisation and it is a small wonder the Tatas have contributed so much in the field of industrial development. Not only this, they paid equal attention to the social side. Many prestigious institutions of the country in the field of fundamental sciences, medicines, engineering, management and social sciences were the result of this attention.

I was overwhelmed by this aspect of the Tatas and it made me draw some deep lessons which I am going to share in this write-up. It reminded me of an interaction of mine with a very senior officer who had retired from the Indian Administrative Service. He is a highly spiritual person and has played a great role in shaping my thinking.

One day I asked him whether at any time he had missed his wish in life and if so how he took it. I was conscious of the fact that missing one's wish was something common and so was more interested in the second part of the question. To this he gave a very interesting reply. He said that on several occasions he did not get what he wished for but what he got in turn was better than what he had wished for. Then he added one condition, that the wish should be selfless and natural. The above principle applied only in case of such a wish. I was quite satisfied with the answer and found it greatly true in my life too.

It is commonly seen that many good people suffer for no apparent fault of theirs. Their natural wishes are also not fulfilled, be it getting a job, getting married, begetting a child, owning a house or winning a promotion. None of them are unnatural wishes. Everyone has a right to get them. But it does not always happen so. There are many instances when deserving persons miss these things in life. What to do in such a situation ? One easier but of course defeatist way is to fret and fume over the missing part of the life. People may listen to them in the beginning but they end up making themselves as pitiable objects. They hardly find any helpers. At best, some people may show sympathy but most of them will turn out to be rejoicers.

The other way is to accept the reality gracefully and to grow larger than the wish. Such are the people who end up getting more than their wish. They expand their vision so much that their own problem becomes too small. They find delight in seeing others getting what they missed themselves. There are numerous examples in the history of mankind when great persons rose above their narrow personal problems to pursue a higher cause. In fact, all great men and women, we talk of, passed through such situations.

J R D was, of course, one of them. The fact that he had no child of his own did not stop him from expanding his vision and looking at the entire mankind as his children. No wonder he laid so much emphasis on the welfare of his employees. He must have always seen them as his children, getting delight in their growth. Who can say that he had no child ? After all, one wants a child mainly to keep the family name going. By this criterion he has numerous children as the family name is not only going but is running smoothly. In fact, the holding company of the Tatas is named Tata Sons.

So when you miss your wish, expand your vision and rise above the wish. Surely you will end up getting more than what you had wished for.

- The man who lives only for himself is a failure. The man who lives for others has achieved true success.
- There is no limit to man's desire, he goes on desiring and when he comes to a point where desire cannot be fulfilled, the result is pain.

50
CONFLICT OF A SAROVAR

Calcutta is a crowded city. Its traffic jams, congested bazars and teeming streets are well known. An outsider, visiting Calcutta for a few days, normally does not have a good impression of the city. Naturally, when on promotion I was offered a posting in Calcutta, I was in a dilemma as I was very comfortably settled in Delhi. An early riser, I like to go either to play tennis or for a long walk in the morning, and in Delhi, I had good amenities for both. The tennis courts were at my doorstep and playing tennis had become a part of my routine. I was not sure of these facilities in Calcutta. Anyhow, considering all the pros and cons, I decided to accept the offer. All my family members also supported the decision, thus reducing my conflict to some extent.

My flat in Calcutta, though very comfortable, was located in a very busy area where it was difficult to find open spaces for morning walks. Though my tennis was arranged within a week of my shifting to Calcutta, I preferred occasional walking. On the very first day, I ventured out on a morning walk and took the direction suggested by the security staff of the building. After walking for about half a kilometre, the area opened out and I found a large number of morning walkers enjoying the fresh air. Soon after, I came across a big sarovar and learnt that it was the famous Rabindra Sarovar. On one side of this sarovar, there stretched a very good road with multi-storey buildings all along, as well as a swimming and a rowing club. By all standards, it was a clean and developed area with no sign of the Calcutta crowd.

The air was quite unpolluted and I was happy at the discovery of such an area which totally eliminated the conflict in my mind about my decision.

For a few days I tried several routes and soon established a pleasant walking route of about forty-five minutes which included a complete round of the sarovar. I followed this direction whenever I went for a morning walk and never felt the need for any change.

I am very contemplative during my walks and many subtle thoughts occupy my mind during this period, particularly, when I am alone. As mentioned earlier, on one side of the sarovar was a clean road lined by high-rise buildings. However, the opposite bank of the sarovar was a totally different picture. The road on that side was very pot-holed and dirty, and very few took this route. A number of people, including women and children, carried out their morning activities on that side of the sarovar, all of them being very poor. Whether they were bathing, washing clothes or utensils, brushing their teeth or excreting, they appeared to be in a state of bliss. They did not seem aware of the fact that the water being used by them was stagnant and its constant use was making it dirtier. Perhaps, they had been doing so for a long time, and the thought of infection or pollution was totally alien to them. I do not think it was easily possible to talk to them about this.

Well, leaving that job to the environmentalists and health workers, I looked at it from a different viewpoint. Here was a sarovar which faced conflicting scenes on its two sides. On one side there was a posh area where the residents tried their best to maintain cleanliness, while on the other side, people blissfully made the area dirtier. Between this conflict, the sarovar itself remained very neutral, allowing its use by the people, the way they did. It remained calm, serene and offered whatever nature ordained it to do. In other words, it was perfectly harmonious in a situation of total conflict.

We all often face such conflicts in life. Some people are happy to see our purity and help us to maintain or increase it, but others exploit us to the hilt and in the process, also try to drag us down. The people in the first category live for higher causes and do not want to hurt anyone or waste their time and energy in skirmishes with baser types. At times, the process is painful but they try to harmonise the two conflicting situations with the help of higher natural forces. Thus, they are able to maintain their harmony, notwithstanding the fact that many keep trying to disturb it.

This is what happened in the case of the sarovar, a symbol of detached high-mindedness. Despite being polluted by many, it maintained its purity. In this process, nature helped greatly as did those people who cared for its purity and cleanliness. Let us hope that this balance will be maintained and the sarovar will continue to remain pure, thus serving the needs of well-wishers as well as neutralising the depredations by exploiters.

Giving and Forgiving

What makes life worth the living
Is our giving and forgiving.

Giving tiny bits of kindness
That will leave a joy behind us.
And forgiving bitter trifles
That the right word often stifles.

For the little things are bigger
Than we often stop to figure.
What makes life worth the living
Is our giving and forgiving.

—Thomas Grant Springer

THE MISSION SONG

Curse not darkness, Light a lamp
Awaken humanity, Which is damp.
Wait not, For that it is dark;
Let thy lamp, Act as a spark
Remove darkness, Awaken humanity;
And restore it, Its dignity.
Curse not darkness, Light a lamp;
Awaken humanity, Which is damp.
Fear not this Mahabharata, Actors are all
Pandava you, they Kaurava; Victory thy goal.
Number their, Makes you undecided;
Search Krishna, To get Gita recited.
Curse not darkness, Light a lamp;
Awaken humanity, Which is damp.
Forget not, They soaked in mud;
Have nothing to offer, But mud.
Keep temper, Get water fast;
For thy victory, Unto the last.
Curse not darkness, Light a lamp;
Awaken humanity, Which is damp.